D0810600

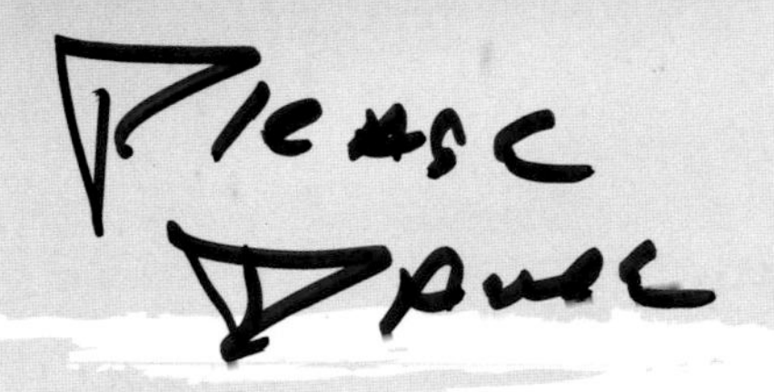

I HOPE YOU DANCE

the power and spirit of song

stories from the John Scheinfeld film

Foreword by Tim Storey

Edited by Judith A. Proffer

I HOPE YOU DANCE

the power and spirit of song

Stories from the John Scheinfeld Film

Edited by Judith A. Proffer

Distributed by Simon & Schuster, New York, NY

Enquiries should be addressed to: Post Hill Press,
275 Madison Avenue, 14th Floor, New York NY 10016 - www.PostHillPress.com

Hardcover ISBN: 978-1-61868-791-3 / eBook ISBN: 978-1-61868-792-0

THE SONG:
Words and Music by Tia Sillers & Mark D. Sanders
Published by Sony/ATV Melody and Choice Is Tragic Music / Universal Music Corp. and Soda Creek Songs

THE FILM:
Produced by Spencer Proffer
Co-Produced by Judith A. Proffer
Executive Producer: Phillipa Sledge
Producers: John Scheinfeld & Dave Harding

Written & Directed by John Scheinfeld

Cover, Interior Design and Illustrations by Hugh Syme - www.hughsyme.com
Art Direction by Judith A. Proffer

Printed in Canada.

For Mark and Tia

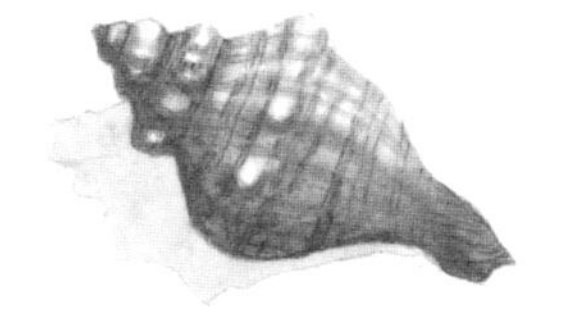

We must accept finite disappointment,
but never lose infinite hope.

– Martin Luther King, Jr.

Foreword

The song "I Hope You Dance," at its very core, asks us to embrace and celebrate the power and purpose of hope. Hope to live. Hope to heal. Hope to trust. Hope to be. And, yes, hope to dance. Why do we require so much hope? Because there will inevitably be pockets of disappointment in life (and sometimes those disappointments are overwhelming and mountainous in nature), but, if we hold on to the idea of hope and all it represents, then we possess the motivation to shift the disappointment to action and, ultimately, to amazement.

Whoever concocted the notion of hope knew what they were doing. It's a tremendous gift that we can present to ourselves—the belief in a steadfast beacon that will carry us through even the most treacherous of storms. And to want hope for others? A loving gesture beyond measure.

To me, this exquisite song is all about moving forward and striving for our best life. It encourages us to never give up and to always participate. To shun the sidelines in favor of standing center stage in our own sphere. Simply put, this song encourages us to turn our setbacks into our comebacks—a message dear to my heart and my life's work.

It's an absolute marvel how music affects many different areas of the brain. It affects the motor cortex, which stimulates movement, foot tapping, and dancing. The brain's nucleus accumbens affects how we react to music emotionally. The sensory cortex processes the tactile feedback we get from playing an instrument and dancing. The auditory cortex handles the perception and analysis of tones when we hear music. When we hear music, our brains engage. We feel, we move, we shift.

Music is not only healing to the soul, but studies have shown that music is also great for treatment in reducing depression, anxiety, and chronic pain. It can produce biological changes, such as reducing heart rate, blood pressure, and cortisol levels. Lyrics can increase positive thought, empathy, and helping behavior. Music stimulates and it heals.

"I Hope You Dance" is so much more than an amazing piece of music. It's an anthem. I suspect that we connect to it so emotionally and deeply because it beautifully speaks our truth.

The line from the song that means the most to me personally is, *"I hope you never lose your sense of wonder."* So often in life, we feel ready to give up and get complacent. We feel so beat up about something that we stop living purposefully and, instead, walk through the motions of everyday life without igniting intent.

"Tell me who wants to look back on their years and wonder where those years have gone." It's just so important to never look back on life and regret what we didn't do, and to instead be joyful of the things that we did do. To always want to learn or try new things. To always stretch our imaginations. To love and be positive even when you feel you are in a dark place. To believe the light is there, welcoming us and expecting us to do the work to get there.

I suppose that's the difference between wishing for something and hoping. Wishing is magical, right? In theory and in definition, a wish kind of happens to you. Hope requires faith; it requires belief; it requires action. It's a message concocted in concert by the heart, soul, and brain. Hope is all sorts of powerful.

And, once you harness the concept of infinite hope, you live, you dance, you soar.

Tim Storey

Los Angeles, California

Time is a wheel in constant motion

always rolling us along.

Music expresses that which cannot be put into words
and cannot remain silent.

– Victor Hugo

Introduction

I often reflect on how fortunate I am to have such a great job. As a documentary filmmaker, I go to interesting places and talk to interesting people about interesting things.

The documentary film, *I Hope You Dance: The Power and Spirit of Song*, is packed with very interesting people saying extremely interesting things. It's about the people who conceived and wrote the song. It's about the people who produced, performed, and had the courage to release a record that didn't neatly follow current musical trends. It's about the millions of people who made it a hit ... and about the millions who have embraced it and been inspired by its message ever since.

Over breakfast one morning with producer Spencer Proffer (who happily brought me on board a project that he'd been incubating for several years), I laid out my vision for the film. By weaving together true stories of how this extraordinary song has motivated real people to transform their lives, to chase their dreams, to overcome obstacles, and to persist in the face of extreme adversity, the film would inspire and empower others to achieve more, to live their best lives.

Our production team uncovered more than a hundred worthy stories before selecting these compelling narratives filled with hope, faith, optimism, and the power of music to inspire and heal. For the next three months we crisscrossed the country—New York, Texas, Tennessee, Arizona, Pennsylvania, Virginia, and North Carolina—to capture these stories for the film. We met amazing people and got to know them as they welcomed us into their lives. Each of the on-camera interviews was special in its own way, but all of our "stars" opened up, sharing their deepest thoughts, feelings, and emotions in remarkably candid ways.

Along the way, I also had the pleasure of sitting down with iconic singer-songwriters Vince Gill, Graham Nash, and Brian Wilson, and talking with them about what it means to create music that has a worldwide following and has significantly impacted people's lives.

And, finally, Pastor Joel Osteen and Dr. Maya Angelou graciously offered us their unique perspectives on the themes explored in the film—Adversity, Aspiration, Second Chances, Recovery, Forgiveness, and Miracles.

There's one clear memory I have of the afternoon we spent at Pastor Osteen's Lakewood Church in Houston. As the crew was setting up, his assistant informed us that Joel's schedule was packed and that we would only have 15 minutes with him for the interview. This was disappointing as I had planned for a good half-hour. Joel arrived and we started. Not surprisingly, it turned out to be a positive and uplifting interview that lasted 45 minutes! After I asked my last question (and a few extra that I slipped in), Joel finally got up and said, "That was fun." But, he didn't rush off. Instead, he stayed even longer to chat with me and the crew. We left Texas very impressed by his warmth, kindness, and, of course, his eloquence. Our film is far better for having him in it.

A few weeks later, Dr. Angelou also captured our hearts. Extraordinarily eloquent, she shared her thoughts on a wide range of topics in addition to "I Hope You Dance," one of her favorite pieces of music. What touched and impressed me so strongly was that, although she was having difficulty breathing (requiring oxygen from time to time) and had to use a walker, she did everything she possibly could to make us feel welcome and to provide a great interview. She even took the time to read the lyrics to "I Hope You Dance" and to share her thoughts about each individual line. At one point, I recall asking her if there was someone specific in the world who ought to listen to the song. She didn't hesitate, saying something to the effect of "Absolutely! I'd love everybody to listen to it and to have a copy of it. There's no one, from the president to the street sweeper, that shouldn't listen to that song and take what he or she needs from it."

While her transcripts don't appear in this volume, poignant footage from our time together is laced throughout the documentary. Such a magical woman! I learned firsthand how very special this song was to her.

This book contains the results of our labors over those many months. The stories you'll find in these pages speak to the song's reach in moving and often surprising ways. The paths that led Mark D. Sanders and Tia Sillers to write it. A homeless woman who reclaimed her life through dance. A quadriplegic whose faith heals her. A father who navigates a parent's worst nightmare. And a reluctant bride who finds her way to happiness with the song as her true north.

You'll meet Evolution of Dance creator Judson Laipply. And Music Therapist Alexandra Field, who offers insight into how and why music moves us, and why this particular song means what it does to so many.

I have no doubt that all of their timeless words will inspire and move you as they did me.

John Scheinfeld
Los Angeles, California

Music is the melody whose text is the world.

– Arthur Schopenhauer

Contents

The Story

Welcome to the world of "I Hope You Dance." A place where music shines, warmly embraces, and even heals. Where hope rides mightily on the wings of melodic poetry. Where wondrous stories abound of a refrain that purposefully and poignantly burrowed its way into hearts and joyfully lifted spirits. A space where comfort, connection and celebration reside and thrive.

It was, at its onset, a dance with serendipity. An unassuming song infused with a bewitching timelessness and an unabashedly optimistic message marked the beginning of a curious new century. Destiny's Child, *NSYNC, Santana, and Madonna were all topping charts in 2000 when "I Hope You Dance" quietly emerged out of Tennessee in March of that same year. The sweetly profound epistle swiftly struck a chord with listeners and had Nashville buzzing. It was a fresh approach to country; it was breathtaking—and it never looked back.

The winsome lyrics and lilting melody combined with Lee Ann Womack's sublime vocals made for unprecedented music magic—quickly crossing over from country to pop and leaving an indelible imprint across the divide. Tia Sillers found inspiration for the song during a purpose-driven beach holiday after a relationship ended badly. Mark D. Sanders brought some personal childhood trauma, adventures in fatherhood, and a seasoned songwriter's wisdom to the mix.

Lee Ann was initially drawn to the song from a mother's viewpoint, a wistful perspective on the things she wished for her own children. The "I Hope You Dance" video, with nearly twenty million views to date, even featured Lee Ann and her then very young daughters, Aubrie Lee and Anna Lise. The song's theme has since taken on a life of its own beyond this parental entreaty—it has become an umbrella of generous words of hope and empowerment, a shield to calm life's chaos and challenges.

The song's producer Mark Wright, one of its great champions, describes hearing "I Hope You Dance" for the first time: "The lyrics in the verses just blew my mind. I thought, 'man I've never heard anything quite like this ...' It was total poetry."

Bruce Hinton, former chairman of Universal Music Group (and current chairman emeritus of MCA Nashville) remembers when Mark Wright delivered the completed track: "There was electricity in the room when it finished. You know, I've been around quite a few hit records in my time, but it was very easy for me to say that this was a slam-dunk No. 1 ... I called Tia at her home and said, 'I think you and Mark have written one of the most important songs not of the year, but forever.'"

Two versions of "I Hope You Dance" were released. The original version was a country song with the band Sons of the Desert singing the chorus alongside Lee Ann. The second was a pop version with background vocals.

Billboard magazine praised the album as a "career record ... years from now, when critics are discussing Lee Ann's vocal gifts and impressive body of work, this is a song that will stand out. It's one of those life-affirming songs that make you pause and take stock of how you're living. It's filled with lovely poetry that will make listeners think."

Leading country music deejay Shawn Parr heard the song early. "When I first heard 'I Hope You Dance,' it just took my breath away," he told filmmaker John Scheinfeld. "There are a lot of songs out there, but there are so few that really grab you the first time you hear them and say, '*Hang on a second—stop and listen to the lyrics of this song.*' It really hit home. The first time I heard it, I knew it was going to be a universal song. Lee Ann came by the station and we talked about the song. She was an amazing interview. We played the song for the first time on the radio in Los Angeles and the phones went crazy. When you have a song that reaches out and grabs people, you know it's going to be special."

In addition to industry nods and fan devotion, "I Hope You Dance" has been widely lauded. In 2001, the song received the Grammy award for Best Country Song. That same year, it was recognized with "Song of the Year" awards from the Country Music Association (CMA); the Academy of Country Music (ACM); Nashville Songwriters Association International (NSAI); the American Society of Composers, Authors And Publishers (ASCAP); and Broadcast Music, Inc. (BMI). The song also reached No. 1 on the *Billboard* Hot Country Singles & Tracks chart and then crossed over to claim the No. 1 spot on the *Billboard* Hot Adult Contemporary Tracks chart.

Dr. Maya Angelou, the late Pulitzer Prize-winning poet, cited "I Hope You Dance" as her favorite song and told Oprah Winfrey, "If I had a daughter—and I feel that you are my daughter—those are the words I would want to say to my daughter." Dr. Angelou sent a CD of the song to Oprah, who then invited Lee Ann to perform the song on *The Oprah Winfrey Show*.

When Dr. Angelou passed away in 2014, Lee Ann paid tribute by singing Dr. Angelou's beloved "I Hope You Dance" at her memorial.

In an interview with *Rolling Stone*, Lee Ann remarked, "... all these years later, the song remained ... That says so much about the power of music and poetry: the way the human condition can be filtered down in a song. Keeping it real and honest, but also maintaining the love in your heart and compassion ... that makes for an excellent life, and that's what I think Maya Angelou found in the song."

Since its release, "I Hope You Dance" has been embraced by numerous musical artists—most notably Gladys Knight, who recorded it for Tyler Perry's 2008 film *The Family That Prays* and in 2014 on her own album, *Another Journey*. Irish singer-songwriter Ronan Keating released a version in 2004 that hit No. 2 on the UK charts. It's long been a contestant favorite on *American Idol*. A video captures a 14-year-old Carrie Underwood singing a stunning version that belies her years. *American Idol*'s first-season winner Kelly Clarkson offered her own powerful take and *I Hope You Dance, The Power and Spirit of Song* producer Spencer Proffer tapped Gospel artist Mandisa (the fifth *American Idol* contestant to win a Grammy) to record a new version of the song for the film.

Search the words "I Hope You Dance" and you'll find a maze of videos. Numbering in the thousands. Among them elaborate montages with the song as soundtrack for weddings, graduations, and virtual scrapbooks of children as they grow. Would-be singing stars offer epic karaoke. Pinterest boards are laced with the lyrics, and over two hundred items related to "I Hope You Dance" are on Etsy's handcrafts webshop, including signs, jewelry, perfume, wall art, clothing, and belt buckles. Chantilly Lane's singing plush collection features the "Hope" bear, dressed in pink cap and shawl with a peppy-tempoed redo of the tune.

Never could songwriters Tia and Mark have imagined the reach and scope of their jewel of a song.

Never could they have ever contemplated a bear singing any of their songs, let alone this one.

And then there are the hundreds of earnest blogs inspired by "I Hope You Dance." Parents whose children are waging health battles share how they derive strength and courage from the lyrics. Dancers who struggle professionally, personally, and physically claim the song as a beacon. And others experiencing varying degrees of adversity offer their own unique kinship with "I Hope You Dance," consistently expressing in tender ways what the song means to them:

How it helped navigate heartache and hardship.

How it connected emotional dots.

And—just as often—how it bookmarked a jubilant moment.

Universally, "I Hope You Dance" is an anthem like few others—one that unites and inspires. A song that flew out of the hearts of its creators, morphing into an entity of flight, carrying its sonorous message on capable wings.

For one design consultant, blogger and mother, "I Hope You Dance" serves both as craft and calling. The song's lyrics command sizable space as custom artwork on a family room wall in her country home. A home she and her family moved to five years ago, far away from the bling and blight of city life after hearing her pastor tell his congregation to "just jump"— and take a chance. Those words spoke to her, and she and her husband transplanted their family for a more conjunctive, peaceful and of the earth way of life. The following post from KariAnne's ThistlewoodFarms.com (www.ThistlewoodFarms.com) blog serves as unfeigned testimony of how, at its root, the song inspires even in the extraordinary ordinariness of everyday life:

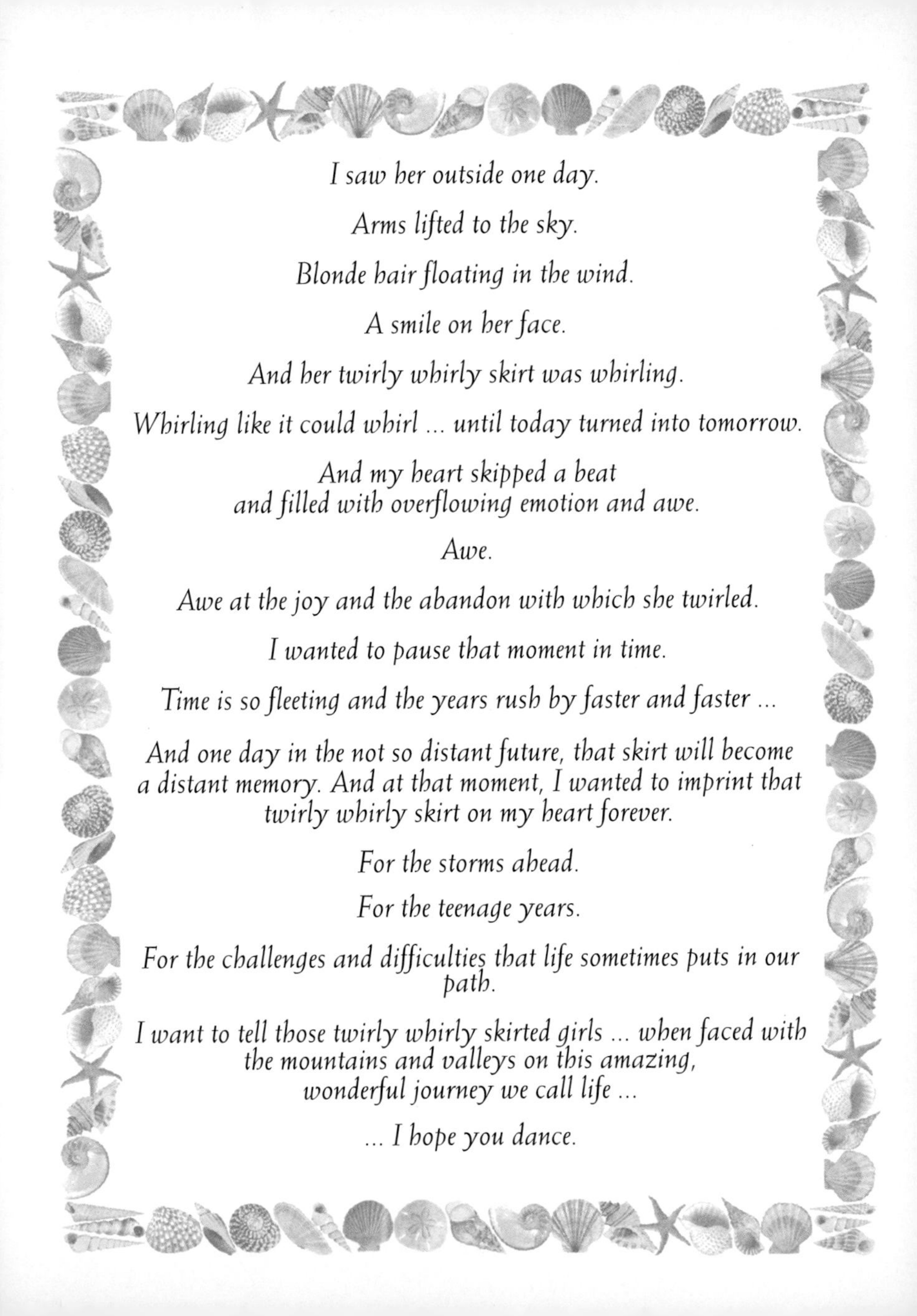

I saw her outside one day.

Arms lifted to the sky.

Blonde hair floating in the wind.

A smile on her face.

And her twirly whirly skirt was whirling.

Whirling like it could whirl ... until today turned into tomorrow.

And my heart skipped a beat
and filled with overflowing emotion and awe.

Awe.

Awe at the joy and the abandon with which she twirled.

I wanted to pause that moment in time.

Time is so fleeting and the years rush by faster and faster ...

And one day in the not so distant future, that skirt will become a distant memory. And at that moment, I wanted to imprint that twirly whirly skirt on my heart forever.

For the storms ahead.

For the teenage years.

For the challenges and difficulties that life sometimes puts in our path.

I want to tell those twirly whirly skirted girls ... when faced with the mountains and valleys on this amazing,
wonderful journey we call life ...

... I hope you dance.

The story of this one precious song from the songwriters' pens to a blogger's wall has been woven with joy, tears, comfort, perseverance, fanfare, amazement, and inspiration. Culminating in John Scheinfeld's impassioned film, it's been a pretty remarkable fifteen-year journey for "I Hope You Dance." The little song that could has become the great big song that did. In reading this book, whether you purchased it or received it as a gift, you're part of that journey. You're part of the "I Hope You Dance" tribe.

You're choosing to harness a sense of wonder.

You're choosing to give faith a fighting chance.

You're choosing to dance.

I hope you still feel small

When you stand beside

the ocean.

Music is a drug.
A mood-altering, totally legal amazing drug with no side effects other than you might accidentally cry or you might feel happier than you wanna feel.
It's crazy what music can do for you...

Tia Sillers

(Singer/Songwriter, "I Hope You Dance" Co-Writer)

I went for a walk on the beach one day—on the state-park side of the beach where there are no cars, no houses, no nothing. I was completely by myself two miles down this beach. I was standing out there, looking at the beach and thinking, "Man, I'm not even a grain in the sand. I'm not even a speck of something. I'm shark bait. I'm nothin'. I am small." It was the most metaphysical I have ever been.

And, all of a sudden, this gigantic black SUV pulled up really fast on the beach, kicking up all this dust. A guy got out, wearing sunglasses and a suit. I imagine him now looking like the David Caruso guy on *Miami Vice*. He whipped out his cell phone and was yelling into it. I remember thinking, "Whoa, this guy doesn't feel small when he stands beside the ocean. And he never will. He's oblivious." I would rather feel like an idiot, an inconsequential grain of sand than be that guy for one stinkin' second.

I was driving back from the beach, all the way back to Nashville. And I was maybe three hours south of Atlanta when my cell phone rang. It was Diana Mayor, one of my best friends and a publisher in Nashville.

"I'm having a writers' retreat with all of my writers out in Colorado starting tomorrow," Diana said. "We just had a cancellation. I know you're on vacation, but we're wondering if your plans have changed."

I told her that I couldn't do it, but she continued to press. "It's a writers' retreat in Colorado, in Estes Park, in the national park there." And, again, I said, "I can't. I've been gone for two weeks and I've got to get back to Nashville."

She pressed some more. "You could come out here and write. Just drive to the Atlanta airport, park your car, and come." And you know, that's what I did. It was the most unplanned thing and it was so great.

I just drove to the airport and bought a ticket that day. This was all before 9/11 and it was easier. It was the first time I had ever seen the Rocky Mountains. I was there for four days and then I flew back to Atlanta, got into my car and drove home. And it was literally the very next day that I wrote with Mark D.

It was serendipitous. Had I not been terrified by those Rocky Mountains or awed by the beach days earlier, I wouldn't have been in that right mindset at all to write with him. It doesn't really matter how creative we are. I had some really seminal experiences, and you can only have so many seminal experiences in your life. I was ready for that writing session. Our meeting had been set up before I left for vacation. I had already canceled a previous one. For this session, though, I came in fresh as a daisy that day, not feeling overwritten or like I was a hamster on a wheel.

The very first time I met Mark D., I was about nineteen or twenty years old. I was babysitting for a songwriter named Alice Randall. She had a little girl that I was taking care of. At that point, I was picking everybody's brains on how to be a successful songwriter. She sent me to her good friend Mark Sanders. And so I went to see him at his office. He met me outside, though, and wouldn't even let me come inside. We stood out on the stoop. I stood there for a while in the rain and made small talk with him.

"Hello, Mr. Sanders, my name is Tia Sillers, and you

ought to write with me," I said. "Here's my cassette." I handed him my songs and I'm sure they were terrible songs. The last thing he said to me that day was, "Yeah, I'll give you a call." And he did, like seven or eight years later. He waited for me to grow up and write some hits. He said it was after I wrote the Dixie Chicks' "There's Your Trouble" that it really got his attention. So he called me up and we got a date on the books.

At that time, he had a teeny little office on the second floor of an MCA building. He's very, very tall—about six-foot-five.

He leaned down toward me. "Hello, Miss Sillers, I'm Mark D. Sanders." He always says that, like he's always just meeting you. Then he said, "I'm on a drug called Effexor. I take Effexor every day. What Effexor does is it puts two little construction workers in my brain, and they go through my brain and they climb up ladders with tacks and a hammer to make sure that the canvas covering the abyss stays up—the tarp covering the abyss."

I thought, "Okay ..."

Then he continued, "As long as I take the Effexor, the construction workers show up. If I don't, the drape covering the abyss comes down."

And, again, I thought, "Okay, well, I get the idea." That was essentially the first thing he ever said to me. And I was hooked. I was hooked on Mark D. Sanders.

He was so difficult and fabulous and confusing and complex and unyielding and flexible. When I got to induct him into the Songwriters Hall of Fame a couple of years ago, I gave a speech and said, "To me, writing a great song, writing with a great songwriter—and with Mark D., in particular—is like we're fencing. It is literally touché, touché, en garde, en garde ...."

I think Mark D. was one of the first people that I ever thought was a worthy opponent—all chutzpah on my part.

The first song we ever wrote together, the day he told me about Effexor, is called, "I Ain't Goin' Nowhere." It got cut immediately and went on a Martina McBride record, so I think he was super inclined to work with me again.

The day we wrote "I Hope You Dance," I had the energy and I felt rested up and fresh. We went to La Hacienda for lunch and, while I was eating avocados and shrimp, I was thinking, "This is a really interesting song, but it's kind of slow and there are lots of words, and no one will ever cut this."

Mark D. is one of the only songwriters in Nashville who loves to take lunch. These days, we all power through—but I don't like to do that. I'm a lover of long crazy lunches where we tell bad jokes, and Mark D. is one of those, too. I do remember that we came up with the line, *"Time is a wheel in constant motion, always rolling us along"* at La Hacienda. Mark D. is the king of craft. The day that we wrote "I Hope You Dance," we bonded and we were together. It was just a great, magical day.

I hardly ever want to write. I never want to write until I'm in the middle of it. Then I get excited. Because, all of a sudden, you think you might be on to something that is magical. There's this period that happens every once in a while when you're writing a song and you think, "This is so great right here." And then comes the finishing and polishing and that's the work.

But there's a little inspirational moment when you think you're onto something—that's the high for me. That's why I keep doing it. I always hope to get to feel that way because it's amazing. There are so many songwriters that I've talked to about this, and they all feel like that. That moment, that crazy moment when you think, "We are amazing." And then it goes away and we think we suck. But, for a moment, we thought we were amazing, and that's great.

Every time I get an idea, I write it in this book and I put different symbols by different ideas, notating the kind of song I think it might be. My husband and I have this saying that the song is king and we're just part of its little fiefdom. I had had the notion of *"If you get the choice to sit it out or dance, I hope you dance"* for a while. And I had actually batted that around to other writers. I had those first couple of lines of *"I hope you never lose your sense of wonder."* It was Mark D. who was so brilliant and said, *"Get your fill to eat but always keep that hunger."* Mark D. grew up really really poor, and I know he was mining that one from there. Have a full belly but always keep that hunger. That line's just golden.

"I Hope You Dance" was a song that just spewed out. Hope and faith are different, and I love hope more than I love faith—because hope covers smaller things. Hope is what makes you wake up in the morning or cross your fingers. Hope is more human, and faith is more spiritual. Hope seems to be more humanly driven, and it's something I always strive to achieve.

This is just one of the songs I have really loved, and I was not prepared for the public's reaction to it. All the songs I've thought were going to be hits have never been hits. And all of the songs that I thought were wonderful but I doubted anybody would ever cut them—those are the songs that have done better.

I was visiting my brother in Seattle when Mark D. made a demo of some songs and decided to add "I Hope You Dance" to the mix at the last minute. A fabulous songwriter in Nashville named Karyn Rochelle sang the song for the demo. Once the demo was wrapped up, it was turned it over to our publishing company.

Our publishing company told us that they loved it, that it was a great demo, and that they wanted to run with it—but they probably say this about every demo. And then, like most songs that a good publishing company gets, they go "Oh, we love it. It's great."

Which they've already said thirty-three times that year so far. And they usually say "We'll run with it." And then they go and knock on some doors and they take the song around and play it for some people. And a number of artists or producers typically say, "No, thank you."

But, with this song, we got a very positive response very soon after we turned it over to them. Pat Finch is an amazing sound guy with just great ears. As a matter of fact, he has "I Hope You Dance" tattooed on his arm, which is kind of bizarre. He doesn't have his wife or kids tattooed on his body, but he's got his biggest song on his arm.

Pat took the song to Mark Wright (Lee Ann Womack's producer) and Mark said he wanted it, and, to prove it, he said that he was going to book a recording session. I don't think he had played it yet for Lee Ann. But, lo and behold, he really did book a session and Lee Ann really did cut it.

Mark Wright was brilliant. He's the one who came up with bringing the line *"I hope you still feel small when you stand beside the ocean"* back toward the end of the song. As songwriters, we didn't have the guts to do that because we were afraid it would make the song too long.

But Mark did what a producer is supposed to do. He took a song that sounded right for his artist and made it sound perfect for his artist. He has ears. He has imagination.

We weren't at the recording session. Songwriters are never invited to that. We are kept so out of the loop that it's shocking.

When I found out that the song was going to be released as a single, I picked up my mom but didn't tell her what the deal was. We drove up these winding Tennessee roads—Tennessee has these gorgeous hills and valleys. We just drove around and I played the song for her over and over again. My mom loved it and was proud of it for me. I was proud of it 'cause I knew she would be proud of it.

I had no sense from anybody at the record company, however, of how they were responding to it. Publishers often won't say anything because so many things go wrong and then you just want to slit your wrist because, after they tell you something's good, then they don't release it. I just can't express how low I am on the food chain.

The song was going up the charts, nice and normal. I was proud of it. All of my songwriting friends were envious of it. But I had no illusions of it being a monster hit or anything.

One day, I was driving from my house toward Music Row in Nashville and every twenty feet were these big green-and-white signs that just had in bold print "I Hope You Dance" over and over again. All the way down the street. And all the way back up. It was so simple and elegant, just the words and that was all. I still have one of those signs.

They told us that the song was nominated for a Grammy. And it just kept getting bigger. People started putting lines from the song on tombstones. Up until then, it just felt like a regular song. I was doing my job. I had written a really good song, and it was an inspiring song. I was proud of it. And I hoped it would go to the Top 10. It never stopped.

I don't really like attention, and I'm not really a person who needs much affirmation. The attention was wonderful and sweet, and I was so happy that it was this song, but the song's success went against my nature. My actual nature.

The song is king. I was just a vehicle for the song. I collect words, I work hard at my craft, but the song is king. By no means am I patting myself on the back. As far as I can tell, it's been played at every father-daughter dance, or mother-son dance at weddings in the history of mankind. In the past decade, I don't think there's been a wedding without it. That's really ironic because it's a very long song. I don't recommend this song as the first dance at weddings because it's hard to dance to.

People have told me that they played the song over and over again while they received chemotherapy. The song has changed people's lives. It has changed mine, too. It has provided tremendous income, of which I've socked most of it away in a bank. And, because I've made some money, I've discovered the ultimate luxury. It's not money. It's not fast cars or mansions. It's time.

I have the time to gaze at my belly button. I have time to notice the colors of the sky each day. I have the time to notice where all of the birds' nests are in my backyard. "I Hope You Dance" has given me the luxury of time.

When I wrote it, I was a lot younger, and, today, when I play it at a show, I will just be completely filled with gratitude for the eloquence of those words. It's basically a list of everything that's probably going to go wrong in your life. I hope it doesn't, but it probably will. There will probably be some idiot hell-bent on breaking your heart and you may wind up bitter for a while. You are probably going to love something and lose. I hope you learn from it. You're probably going to fear those mountains in the distance. You're probably going to settle for the path of least resistance. You're probably going to do those things. And they're going to hurt you. I still hope, in spite of all that, even in the ashes, even in the drought, even in the dry well, even with the busted lip and the black eye, I hope you say, "I think

I'll dance" because what other choice do you have? You're here on this earth, and you were born for better or worse, and you will live 'til you die. I hope you get to dance a little bit through it. I think this is the reason why people have been drawn to this song the most. It's not about hoping that everything is rosy and wonderful, and that you meet a boy named Tommy, have 2.5 children, and live in a house with a white picket fence.

Things are probably going to crack your heart a little bit and give you a bunch of scars. But the message is: Rise from the ashes. Shimmy. Tango. Jive. Shake.

The verse in the song that still gets me today is "*When you come close to selling out, reconsider.*" That has been my mantra. And not even selling out, I replace those words with other things. When you come close to spewing vitriol, reconsider. When you come close to kicking a guy in the nuts, reconsider. When you come close to throwing food in the chef's face, reconsider. When you come close to rolling your eyes, reconsider. I believe the majority of the world is trying awfully hard to be good and fairly decent.

The message in "I Hope You Dance" still dictates my life. I have the legacy of "I Hope You Dance" to kinda live up to. I just can't become a schmuck. I wrote "I Hope You Dance." I have to be nice to people.

FAITH

I didn't grow up on country music.
I grew up in Southern California listening
to the Lettermen, the Beach Boys, and Motown.
The first music that inspired me was
"Sgt. Pepper's Lonely Hearts Club Band."

Mark D. Sanders

(Singer/Songwriter, "I Hope You Dance" Co-Writer)

Music is a drug, and it's the drug I used when I was growing up. I was in a very difficult situation. My family fell apart when I was seventeen, and music got me through it. I went up in my room, and I listened to music and I played my guitar. I tried to learn songs and it got me through. Music is powerful. When life is ugly, music can still be beautiful. I think about hymns, when you're in a big church service and everyone's singing the same thing. There's just something in there. I write from my own life, and I've written from my own life for many years. When I do write from my own life, it's definitely more powerful. But I have to be careful that it's not just for me. I can only talk about my life so many times before it starts getting boring. If I can take something from my life and put it into a song, and have some truth, then I think the song is more powerful.

Part of the reason I'm a songwriter is that I've dealt with depression my whole life. It made me almost incapable of holding a regular job. I have this wonderful brother who's a year older. He has worked for Jostens Yearbooks for thirty-five or forty years. He's the same guy every day. I've realized that I'm a different guy. It depends on my state of mind. So I had to be a songwriter, where you can go to lunch whenever you want to.

The hard part when you're a songwriter is that you're trying to get somebody else to sing your words, to say your words, and you want it to be true for them. It's easy to write a song, but it's difficult to write a song that someone else can sing and have it be true for them.

My goal as a songwriter is for somebody else to take my song and make something of it. I love that it becomes Lee Ann Womack's song or it becomes George Strait's song. I get to deal with anonymity. When I walk into a record store, I'm not Lee Ann Womack walking into the record store. I'm just the anonymous guy who wrote the song. I know music connects the artist to the audience.

"I Hope You Dance" was written before 9/11. And we

were all more connected back then. I think that, after 9/11, we got divided. The whole world got divided into this faction and that faction. "I Hope You Dance" is a pre-9/11 song. It connects people. For years, I've told people that *"I hope you . . ."* are the most important words in the song because it's me talking about what I hope for you. And everybody in the audience thinks the singer is talking to them personally.

My older sister wanted to start a Montessori Middle School. The first time I saw her after the song came out, she said, "Mark, do you know what you've done?" Apparently, I had convinced her to start this school because of the song. There are times when you write really great songs and times when you write lousy songs, and, in Nashville, everyone will tell you which ones are lousy.

So the first time I met Tia Sillers, she had called and wanted to write with me. My career was just taking off. I had my first No. 1 record and I was thrilled. My motto in songwriting was "keep your eye on the prize." You know, don't get sucked in to some side channel, trying to write artsy songs or something. Well, this young woman called me. She came to my office, but I wouldn't let her in the door. I stood outside and talked to her and looked at the tapes she had brought me. She told me who she had written with. She was only about twenty, and I guess I was in my mid-thirties then. I didn't know anybody else named Tia. I thought, "Tia, I don't know that I really want to get into this right now," and so I just said, "Let me just listen to it and I'll get back to you."

It took me about seven years but I did finally get back to her. I followed Tia's career and heard songs she had written. I had had a whole bunch of success and was just kind of coasting, so I said to my song plugger, "Let's call Tia Sillers. I think I'd like to write with her." I had this odd talent of being good at writing with women who talk a lot.

When Tia and I meet, she'll just start talking about whatever it is we're writing about, and I'll sit there and listen until I hear a word that sounds like it belongs in the song. Tia Sillers is this dynamo, this redheaded dynamo, who is just full of ideas and life. She's the opposite of me. I'm this quiet guy who's pensive. If Tia's pensive, you know about it. With me, you don't know. Tia's just like a miracle.

She came to me after she had been at the beach for a couple of weeks and she was going through a tough time in her life. I was just being a songwriter, waiting for her to get back. She came in with five or six ideas and she read them to me. The idea that hit me was the one about dancing. I said to her, "Let's write this, the dance one."

She had the very first line of the song, *"I hope you never lose your sense of wonder"* and then she had a line *"I hope you always keep that hunger."* When I was a kid, I went through a tough time and I was hungry. I thought, "God, I don't want anybody to be hungry." So I said, "Tia, that line has to be something more than it says."

The song crafter in me came up with the line *"You get your fill to eat but always keep that hunger."* That says what I want it to say. It does it in a great way. It has a little rhyme inside it and the line feels great.

That's what co-writing is—her life and my life trying to make a song—and every line is almost like a Hallmark card. Some lines mean more to her than they do to me. Each line was an adventure. A song is shaped by its rhymes. That's just how it works. There's a science to rhyming. Rhyming gives you comfort, just like the song gives you comfort.

The song's *"I'll give the heavens above more than just a passing glance"* is a nice line, to think about God and your spiritual side, but it also rhymes with "dance." My favorite two lines have always been *"Living might mean taking chances but they're worth taking."* After we wrote that line, I thought "You know I know what the next line needs to say. I wonder if it will fit." So we said, *"Loving might be a mistake but it's worth making."* Is love worth making or is the mistake worth taking? It just fit. It was like God shining down on us, saying, "Yes, you can say what you want to say."

To me, that was the crowning line. I just thought, "If we can say that, we can do anything." We were at lunch that day—and Tia has some concept that we were at one restaurant but I'm sure she's wrong, that we were at another restaurant—and we wrote the lines, *"Time is a wheel in constant motion, always rolling us along. Tell me who wants to look back on their years and wonder where those years had gone?"*

I had written stupid country songs. That's where I made all my money. Here, we just got to say what we wanted to say, and it was her life and my life and the music fed us. It just all came out in one song. I had no clue whatsoever that it was going to be a big song because I never had any success with stuff like this. It didn't take very long to write the song, maybe a day and a half. We came back the second day and cleaned up some lines, but it didn't take very long.

It never seemed like it was going to be a story song. It was just a song where I'm talking to you and I'm hoping these things for you. When I was twenty-nine, I had a choice—although it didn't feel like I had a choice. I was in California surfing every day and working whatever job I could. I loved being in the ocean and thought, "I've got to leave this and be a songwriter. That's very painful." It killed me the first couple of years, but, if you get the choice to sit it out or dance, I hope you dance. So I danced in my life. I think Tia danced. I know, for my kids, when they get the choice, I encourage them to dance. To go do it. Even if it doesn't work, go do it, try it.

After we had written the song, Tia was out of town for something and I had some songs I needed to demo where we'd go into the studio and hire musicians and singers and try to make it sound like a record. One day, Tia's publisher came to my office, which is very unusual. I've known him for a long time but he would never come to my office. He said, "Mark, I want you to take extra care with this song."

I asked him what I should do with it. "Make it sort of alternative sounding in the demo," he said. I thought about that. I didn't have any grand plan. I'm not the greatest demo producer. At the studio, when we were laying down the tracks, the guitar player, J.T. Corenflos, was playing the song with more of a country feel. I asked J.T. to play it with more of an alternative sound, as Tia's publisher had suggested, and so J.T. played the guitar like you hear on the record.

I recorded five songs on the demo that day, and then I took them to my song pluggers, who are the salespeople in this business. After hearing "I Hope You Dance," they said, "We're going to run with this one." And they did.

I was disappointed that, out of five songs that I was

hoping would be five hits, they only wanted one. They took that song and played it for producers, record guys, and artists. It went on hold for Lee Ann Womack. I knew Lee Ann, and she had sung demos for me. And I knew Mark Wright, her producer. I heard through other people that Mark was going to take great care of this song. I never want to be in the studio once somebody's recording my song. I separate myself. I write a song and demo it, and then I try to give it away. I really don't want to be involved after that.

After Lee Ann had recorded "I Hope You Dance," I heard from Bruce Hinton, the head of MCA Records. He said, "Mark, I know I don't call you very often," and I said, "Bruce, I'm fifty years old and you've never called me." And he said, "I feel like we're going to have this big record and I want us to be in communication on it because I feel like we're going to win a bunch of awards."

I thought, "I've always wanted to win awards ..." He then said, "The reason I have been able to keep this job is that I'm good at anticipating what records are going be big, and I think this is one of them." And I thought, "Man, I love the sound of that."

It can be very stunning to hear one of your songs in the recorded form with the artist's voice. It can drive you to tears or you can just go "Whoa. That's a voice I know." Lee Ann has such a voice. It's a wonderful feeling. Lee Ann's version of the song will always be my favorite.

I've heard Gladys Knight sing it, and it took me to a whole new place. I've heard people sing it on You Tube in front of a mirror. I've heard a million people sing it. Carrie Underwood, *American Idol*. I've heard Lee Ann sing it live with just a guitar and have just been blown away.

When the record came out, I felt like we were headed somewhere. I could tell. It was just so different from anything I had experienced. I was feeling pretty good and I ate it all up. My wife says I got a little big-headed about it, which is probably true. I had so much wanted to write a song that won some awards, and I was just so excited about that prospect. When we got nominated for a Country Music Association (CMA) award, that was the first time I'd ever been nominated. I thought, "You can't beat that."

I knew we'd get to go to the CMA Awards. I bought a new car, thinking that, if I'm going to valet my car at the CMA Awards, I need to have a nice car, no old Jeep. It was just great. A wonderful time. We won a Grammy, and that was just another unbelievable thing in my life. I think about my mother, who died in 1994, and she just wouldn't have believed it.

I was born in Los Angeles in 1950, and we were just a struggling hardly middle-class family. I was born about a mile from the Staples Center, where I came back and won a Grammy. You talk about weird circles and that was it right there. So I got a big head. The song changed my life. I had come to Nashville and had made a chocolate sundae—and then to win a Grammy and other Song of the Year awards... that was all frosting on the cake.

The funny thing about it is that the song is not me. And I am not the song. Tia's mom got mad at me one night because I said something and she replied, "Well, that's not how your song talks about life." I said, "Well, I'm not the song. I'm me." The song changed my life, but it didn't change me. I don't think this song would have changed my life if I was just hearing it, if I hadn't written it. It's not necessarily the kind of song that takes me places. For twenty years, I wrote songs for a living. I got to kind of back away a little and relax a little bit. I started writing songs more the way I did when I first got here, more personal.

After we wrote "I Hope You Dance," Tia and I would get back together and write again. One time, we wrote a song that was sort of like "I Hope You Dance." It was a powerful song and philosophical in a way. We made a really nice demo and we got this woman to sing the demo who just made the song better. I took it to my song plugger, who said, "It's really good, but it's no 'I Hope You Dance.'"

I thought, "Holy smokes, what have I gotten myself into?" The first 2,000 songs I wrote in Nashville weren't "I Hope You Dance" either. There aren't more "I Hope

You Dance" songs because they just don't get written. We wrote it.

It's not easy being the guy who wrote "I Hope You Dance," but it's fun.

Hope is the belief that there is something better in the future. It's so important that we have hope because, if you don't have it, that's when you stop living. You just start existing

Joel Osteen

(Pastor, Author)

I believe that, in life, we all face obstacles. And sometimes we see them as randomly happening and they're just going to defeat us and then we get discouraged. When you get your hopes up and you know that your greatest victories are ahead of you, that gives you great purpose to get out of bed in the morning.

I think there's a purpose for everything. There are a lot of things that we don't understand, especially as a pastor. I meet people here that have cancer and life-threatening diseases. I can't say that I understand it all, but part of faith is trusting God when you don't understand it. If we could figure it all out, we wouldn't need faith. There are many instances where we can go as far as our education, but that's not far enough. We need supernatural breaks and to meet the right people, and that's when faith comes in.

Sometimes life pushes us down and it's easy to stay down. We look up and think, "How can I rise out of this environment? How can I move forward?" I believe you have to get up on the inside. If you can see it on the inside, I believe that's what helps God bring it to pass on the outside. But many people have lost their inner vision. I don't think you'll ever rise any higher than how you see yourself. And when you get stuck in a situation and think, "Well, it's going to be more of the same." That's what limits us.

You have to know there's a second chance. You keep moving forward. You have seeds of greatness on the inside, and every one of us is destined for a purpose. And that purpose is not to get stuck where we are, but rather it's to rise up and out of any situation and to move forward. I see so many people getting stuck because they carry baggage from yesterday into today. Whether it's twenty minutes ago that something happened or sometimes it's twenty years ago. People beat themselves up from mistakes they've made or they may be mad at somebody else or they didn't have the right childhood or there are many excuses we could all come up with. I believe you have to let every day be a new beginning. Life is not always fair. But I believe God is always fair.

I've met some people that have had terrible pasts, but they just move forward. They let go of their mistakes. They let go of what didn't work out. You *have* to let go. You have to let go of the questions. You have to let go of the things you don't understand.

Music creates feeling and emotion, and it's a big part of our services because it gets your heart ready to receive. The right music is very powerful. We can create feeling and emotion, and I do feel like music and worship and praise get your heart ready to receive. The line from "I Hope You Dance" that says, *"I hope you never lose your sense of wonder"* says to me that we should live each day as a gift. We should be amazed at the simple things in life. You get up in the morning and you hear the birds chirping or you hear your children walking down the stairs—or just being able to see your friends and family. I think it's so important that we don't take these things for granted. Each day is a gift and, when we appreciate it like that, that's when we really live it to the fullest.

Which leads to the line *"May you never take one single breath for granted."* It's so important because we often don't realize how fragile life really is. We're here for a moment and there's no guarantee of tomorrow. And sometimes we treat our relationships and even the days as though we're always going to be here. When you realize "today could be my last day," we live it differently. Don't just endure life—enjoy the day. And I love the phrase *"Whenever one door closes, one more opens."* So often, we come to roadblocks in life and we think, "Wow, life's never going to be as good as it used to be." It's easy to get bitter. It's easy to get down and think, "I've seen my best days." But I've found that, if you'll just keep moving forward, there will be another door opening. Another relationship. Another opportunity. The key is don't get stuck where you are; keep moving forward and you'll see that new door open.

"Promise me you'll give faith a fighting chance" means don't give up hope. Keep believing that something good is in your future. It's easy to get negative. It's easy to get discouraged and think "this is all there is," but, when you have faith, it's never over.

"I hope you never fear those mountains in the distance" says don't be afraid to take a risk. Don't be afraid to move forward. There may be some big obstacles, but I believe that we're equipped and empowered

for everything that comes our way. We've been armed with strength to accomplish our dreams.

"Never settle for the path of least resistance" is so important and so true. It's easy to just get into our comfort zone and take the easy way out. But that's never where you're going to see your true fulfillment.

I think we're always supposed to be growing, and resistance is what causes us to develop and grow, and to see the good things that God has in store. You have to be up for the challenge. You have to dig your heels in. You have to move forward, knowing that this thing is not going to defeat me; I'm going to overcome.

I don't think anything we go through is a waste. I say it like this:

Nothing happens *to* you; it happens *for* you.

I hope you get your fill to eat,

but always keep that hunger.

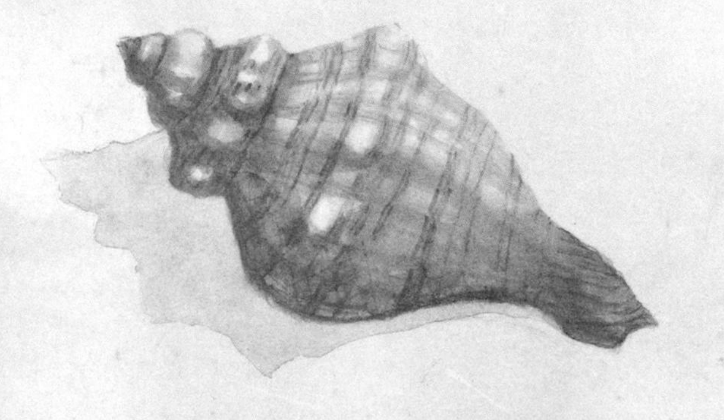

I will dance until physically I can't.
And then I'll be dancing in the spirit world.

Shannon Felty

(From Homelessness to Ballroom Dance)

My dad named me after a dog in a song. *"Shannon is lost. I heard she drifted out to sea."* I was twenty-five years old when I contracted human parvovirus. The phone rang while I was waiting to hear what was wrong with my joints, and, when I answered, the doctor told me that I had parvo. And I said, "Isn't that a dog disease?" A week later, I was in the hospital, dropping weight and unable to keep food down. My illness now included a stomach infection. It was literally just like a dog dying from parvo. I called my dad and said,

"Thanks a lot. This is all your fault. If you wouldn't have named me after a dog, I'd have been healthy."

I am one of a core group of five siblings. I have twelve siblings, but grew up with four others. My mother had five children from two different marriages. We grew up in a household that was chaotic on the best day. And we had a stepfather who was a heroin addict. There was some sexual abuse, and, at a very early age, I noticed that money was the No. 1 issue. Is there going to be food on the table tonight? Are we going to have clothes for school? Can we even afford a notebook? I grew up like that, with constant fear and always noticing that I was not one of the people that "has." I was a "have not." It was really hard to maintain friendships because I always felt like I was beneath other people.

I made my mind up in high school that I didn't have to be that. I could be anything that I wanted to be. And so I became this determined "I'm-not-going to-live-this-way" kind of girl. When I graduated from high school, I moved out of the low-income neighborhood where I grew up and I never wanted to go back.

I couldn't afford college, but, with determination, I found my niche in retail and I moved up into management really quick. I thought that was what I was going to do the rest of my life. I was going to be in senior management in retail.

I became this overachiever. I had to be better than everyone else. I had to be better than I felt I was raised to be. In my early twenties, I had a son. Retail did not include a schedule that I wanted to keep, being a new mom. I was working sixty hours a week and it was a salaried position. I was making less per hour than my sales girls who were working part-time.

So I left retail and went into office work, where I excelled. I became an office manager in an audio visual company. Some things happened there that brought back my childhood for me—things I had tried to forget for so long. Physical touching … gross emails …. I was the only woman and my job became increasingly difficult. So I quit that job and was unemployed for a few months. But I'm very resourceful. I decided I would be a traveling Gal Friday. I was twenty-six at this time. I put an ad in the online community, and, with the economy tanking and so many small businesses having to let go of staff, I figured I could go into a business once a week, twice a month—however much they needed—and do their filing, help them catch up on payroll, and stuff like that.

It afforded me a good few months of setting my own schedule and still having the income. I signed up with a temp agency that put me into an aerospace company in the company's purchasing department while a lady there was out on maternity leave. I was only there to do the bare basics, such as answer phones and greet people at the door. I started learning, on my own, what was going on around me, and I started playing around on the system while I was on lunch.

About four months later, the lady who had been out on maternity leave came back to work, but I kept a purchasing job in that company, which was quite a feat because I didn't have a college education. Most of their purchasing clerks did have college educations.

Life was really good. I thought I had everything I needed. I was in a long-term relationship. I had my son. I was raising another child in that relationship, along with my son, so I had my two boys. My relationship was stable and I was making plenty of money. And my boyfriend was making plenty of money. We didn't want for anything. Not as a family. Not as individuals. Anything we wanted, we pretty much had. And I thought that I'd finally arrived. I had made it in life. I was not the poor girl from the 'hood anymore. I was a successful career woman.

Then I started having a lot of severe aches and pains in my body. I went to doctor after doctor, emergency room after emergency room. They couldn't figure out what the problem was. It was joint pain. It was muscle pain. It was headaches. It was fatigue. They did minor blood tests, took lots of MRIs and CAT scans, and nobody could figure out the problem. I think, eventually, the medical community thought I was drug seeking. The pain was so extreme that I was missing work.

It was difficult to get up out of bed. It was difficult to take care of my kids. I was missing a *lot* of work. I got a warning that, if I missed any more work, then they would have to fire me. So I decided I was just going to struggle through the aches and pains and go to work every day.

But my performance was suffering, and that was really hard for me mentally because I was an overachiever. So here I was in this position in life where I didn't know what was wrong with me; nobody could find what was wrong with me. Someone suggested that maybe it was psychosomatic. I bought into that and checked myself into a behavioral health clinic. I thought, "I have depression issues and I have some anxiety issues, but who wouldn't with the type of lifestyle I had as a child?"

The people that were at the clinic were so different than I was. I didn't have the issues they had. I felt like I was dealing fairly well with my childhood. So then I decided I wasn't crazy.

I got out of there and went to a doctor that was recommended by a friend, and this doctor thought maybe my problem was fibromyalgia. That's a diagnosis I hear a lot now, but, back then, I'd never heard of it. However, the doctor did a pressure point test on me and decided that I didn't have it.

"So maybe I *am* crazy," I said to the doctor. And she said, "Let me take a few blood tests." I told her that blood tests had been run before on me. She replied, "Let me take some specific ones. I'm looking for something."

She did some blood tests, and, two weeks later, she told me, "You're not crazy. You have lupus." I said, "Well, then, give me a pill, and I'll go back to work. My life will be great again." And she said, "It doesn't really work like that. I can give you medication that might help, but your life is going to be different." I asked, "Different how?" and she replied, "You're going to have to take it easy ..."

Lupus is an auto-immune disease. My immune system recognizes my healthy cells along with the diseased cells, and it works overtime to get rid of them. This means that my immune system literally attacks my joints and muscles, and causes inflammation and pain. When I get sick, I get very sick because my immune system works so hard for so long, then it kind of quits for a while. And if I catch anything in that period of time, I'm down for the count. While other people might get a cold and be down for three days, I might be down for a week and a half.

So that changed things. My doctor said I needed to take it easy and learn how to relax. I thought that maybe I would start knitting or something—I had never done that before. My boyfriend suggested that I should quit my job.

I said, "I'm not quitting my job. I love my job." I didn't love my job, but I loved the success I thought I had. I loved the money. I loved proving everybody wrong. I was not going to be this poor little girl from the 'hood. I was successful.

So I went back to work, and it seemed that the more I thought about having to relax, the less I could relax. It was at the forefront of my mind and stressing me out a little bit too much. I really stressed myself into being sick. Stress is a huge trigger for symptoms and flare-ups. So I went back to the doctor, and she said, "How are you doing with this? How's the medication? And what are side effects are you experiencing?"

I said, "I'm doing fine, except that, now that you've told me, I'm sick, I'm really sick."

We talked for an hour about my life—not about the disease but about my stresses. She asked me what I did for relaxation and fun. Fun? I didn't have hobbies. I had children. I didn't have fun. I had a career. I really wasn't taking care of me. I went home from that doctor's visit and talked to my boyfriend. We decided together that maybe I should give up my career. He made plenty of money, and I could stay home and be with the kids. The overachiever in me thought, "Now I can be a PTA mom and a soccer mom." I continued to stress myself out even after that. And, of course, I stayed sick.

About three years into the diagnosis, my boyfriend had a new career in the hotel business. It was in management. Drinking was what you did with clients, and it was how you schmoozed and won over business. He began to drink very heavily. I begged him and begged him to stop.

I stayed because of the kids. I couldn't imagine giving up his son. At that point, I'd raised him for nine years. So he was my kid, too. I knew that, if the relationship dissolved, I would probably not see my common-law stepson anymore. My justification for staying was also that, while my boyfriend might be mean, and verbally and mentally abusive, he still hadn't hit me. And he didn't hit the kids, so I stayed.

I was miserable, and kept getting sicker. And then the stress of my illness and finances came to a boil. One night, my boyfriend came home and he'd been drinking. I was asleep on the couch. He pulled me off the couch by my hair and told me to go to bed. I couldn't believe that, after ten years, this would happen to me. I had watched my sister go through some abuse in her marriage. I didn't want to be that way. As a child, I had also watched my mom get beat up. So I made the decision that night that I had to go.

And, if it meant giving up my stepson, then I had to do that. And I did. But I didn't know where I was going to go. I had no job. I had terrible health. And I had my son. That night, I ended up on my sister's couch with my son. And I had taken my stepson to my sister's house because I had called the cops on my boyfriend and he went to jail for the night. He told the police that he wanted his son to stay with me, so I went to the house to get clothes for the children, as they had to go to school the next day.

When I got to the house, the police were there with representatives from Child Protective Services. They took my stepson away from me. My boyfriend's ex-wife had filed a restraining order against me, claiming that I was a danger to my stepson and that I had kidnapped him. It was the last time I saw him.

I still had my son to live for, but losing my relationship and my stepson was a huge blow. It was a lot to take in. I went to my sister's house and called my ex-husband and said, "You can't just be the fun dad anymore." I sent my son to my ex-husband. He's my best friend, by the way. I'm so fortunate about that.

I couch surfed for about a year, with siblings and friends. Once it got to the point where I felt like I was a burden, I had to find something else to do for my own peace of mind. Nobody kicked me out, but it was hard for them to take care of an adult with a chronic illness, who, day in and day out, is not doing well. I think that would be hard on anybody.

So, after a year of that, I decided that I really needed to make a decision and jump on it. I didn't want to be homeless. Nobody *wants* to be homeless. I had filed with Social Security for disability and that's a long process. In the state of Arizona, it can take 18 to 24 months to process this claim. In my mind, this meant that I would be homeless for 18 to 24 months, so I ended up on a Human Services campus in a shelter system.

I thought that I would be different from the other homeless people that I saw in the system. I was homeless for now, but it was not going to take me long to get back on my feet because I didn't have a mental illness and I didn't abuse drugs or alcohol.

At the same time, I felt like a complete and utter failure. I had spent all of my adult years building up this career-woman supermom persona. When I became homeless, even though I had made the choice to jump into that shelter system, I felt a strong sense of failure. When you become homeless, you don't trust yourself. You don't trust others. You buy into the stereotypes and stigmas that you've seen your whole life. Immediately upon becoming homeless, I felt I was less than human.

There was a roomful of women at the shelter, and they weren't all crazy. They weren't all alcoholics. And they weren't all drug addicts. Maybe it should have made me feel better about myself, but it actually made me feel worse. If they're all in the shelter system, what shot did I have of getting out of there quickly? It was Sunday, and we were locked in. We were, unfortunately, treated like prisoners.

On my first Monday morning there, they dropped us off at the Human Services campus. I'd never heard of the place. It looks like a college campus. It was welcoming, but I was still very fearful. I didn't walk through any of the doors to any of the buildings that first day. I sat outside with my book and tried to ignore everybody around me, which is really hard for a woman to do in a situation like that. It was scary that first day to be a woman and to be in an environment where there are shady things going on around you. I grew up in a low-income environment, and I was street smart, so I guess that worked to my advantage. I just kept to myself and wondered what I was going to do to get out of that situation.

The shelter's services are very broad. I was a high school graduate, so I didn't need GED classes. I couldn't work, so I didn't need job-searching assistance. I just needed my disability paperwork to come through.

Somebody told me that I needed to get involved. Get involved? "What about dance class?" someone suggested. And I said, "Dance class? We're homeless. We're supposed to be figuring out how not to be homeless. I don't have time for dance class. That's frivolous."

So I watched these people go in and out of this classroom every day and come out with smiles on their faces. And I thought, "That's nice, but these people are going to be homeless in a year because they're choosing to dance instead of looking for a job."

One of the dance instructors, Mike Tapscott, walked by me on the campus one day and said, "The next dance session starts Monday. You're going to be there, right?" And I said, "Nope." And he said, "Well, what else are you doing?" Nothing. I was waiting. I didn't even know what I was waiting for, but I was doing nothing. So I said, "Okay, I'll come once."

I went to that first dance class, a ballroom dance class, and I encountered the energy and the smiles—not something I was used to seeing on people's faces around there.

If I never danced a step, that would have been good enough. It was amazing to watch the dancers get it, and to see them be proud of themselves for getting it. It was amazing to see the transformation of these people. These were people, just like me, who didn't trust themselves. They had made bad decisions. They had been with the wrong people or had been abused, or maybe they had drug or alcohol issues. But, in that room, they were just people dancing with others.

Then I started noticing the change in me. And in how I felt about myself. And it wasn't because I was learning to dance. It was about that one hour of fun in my day being what I looked forward to every day. And when I walked out of that room and I had been smiling for an hour, the whole rest of my day just went well. It was this feeling that I had my dignity back. I had my self-respect back. I was not viewed by the people in that room as anything other than a person.

Anywhere outside of that room, I felt like a homeless person. Like a label that was holding me down. And I needed to spend that hour with people who were just being people. So, after the first eight weeks, I kept going back. And what I noticed was that everybody I had seen go through that dance class were the ones who got out and lived life. They were not on the campus anymore. And, if they did return to this campus, it's because they came back to work there or they came back to volunteer and help others. I decided that I was going to be one of those positive stories.

Dancing became the one thing that allowed me to not pay attention to the stresses of having to get out of this situation. It was the one thing that let me have joy. I was free-floating. Laughing. Smiling. And watching others having fun. For that one hour a day, it was that one thing that let me forget about almost every obstacle that I was facing. It became the reason I got up in the morning. For that one hour a day, it didn't dawn on me that I was homeless and living on the Human Services campus. And when you shed all those stigmas and stereotypes that are holding you down, even for that one hour a day, you start to really know who you are inside. Who you were meant to be. This is me, and this is me at my best. I can be at my best even when I'm at my worst.

And it was this kind of magical "aha" moment that I needed. You get rid of everything that's bogging you down. And when you shed all that, you're you. It's the best person to be. I don't have to be a super mom. I don't have to be career driven. I don't have to have money or a car. I'm good all by myself. All by myself. I don't need anything to validate that. I feel good, which means I am good. Even if I were tripping all over myself in that dance class, I still would have felt good about myself when I walked out of there.

My favorite dance is the tango because you can be feminine and strong, and the two don't work against each other. They work with each other and I love that. It's the concept of "I'm allowing you to stalk me, but I can put a wall back up if I need to." It's a power thing. I grew up with a mother who was in a codependent relationship, but I viewed her as strong because she always made things work. I thought that "strong" meant you could take care of the world. And dancing taught me that "strong" means you are taking care of you.

Through the dance class, I got to know Mike Tapscott a lot more. The biggest goofball I've ever met in my life outside of myself. He really has a knack for meeting you where you're at. He doesn't need to know your life story. He's got this knack for literally giving you what you need just enough to hook you in.

He was talking to me about the Just B B Just Soap Company. He said, "You should come volunteer if you're ever looking for something to do. Just come volunteer."

So I showed up one day, and they showed me the soap that they sell. They explained that it wasn't just a soap company. It was a program, and it was just getting on its feet. Ultimately, it is designed so people can learn how to run a company. They don't just make and sell products, they market them and they do financials reporting. And if you have never been around a computer in your life, they'll train you.

They didn't have any women working in the company, so I thought they could definitely use a woman's touch. It was a beauty products company without a woman in it. How was that possible? So I started hanging out and doing whatever I could do. I noticed that they had a little display in a conference room and there were just a few bars of soap scattered on it. I thought that I could make a better display than that. I asked if I could redo the display case and was told, "Have at it." I used to do window displays when I was in management and retail. I'd never worked with soap before, but retail is retail and customers want to see what makes eyes pop.

I went into the soap closet and started pulling product, setting up the display case. I hadn't done a display in so long. I hadn't tapped into my creative energy in years. It was fun. It fed the need in me to be creative.

The more I hung out there, the more I did whatever needed to be done and the more I started noticing where I could fill in the blanks. I came from a purchasing background and a retail background, and felt I could help on so many levels. This was something useful that I could do with my time. So, as a volunteer, I would come and wrap soap if it needed to be wrapped, and I would take a look at things they were doing for computer training. If I could help somebody on the computer, I was there to do that.

It was a source of pride, and not just ugly stubborn pride. More like a feeling that I was worthy, and that I was worth something and was valuable. They hired me as an employee and immediately got me into low-income housing. They encouraged me every step of the way. And it felt natural to keep moving forward.

So I am in housing with roommates now and I'm an accounts manager. I work part-time for Just B and I also work a few hours a week for the Human Services department doing community outreach and helping other individuals who were experiencing homelessness. I see my son as much as possible. My life is very full now and it's not full of just me. And I think that keeps me really focused on the important things in life. It is not about the money. It is not about clothes. It is truly about helping people. That feels really good to me.

I was homeless for over a year. It was not the ideal life. I didn't even know what my ideal life was anymore because it had changed from what it used to be. But I was working toward something better and I felt that every day. I hadn't felt that before.

This is the part of my story where I really cry. My siblings and I found my half-brother, Shawn, who was the oldest of my father's children. We did not grow up together. He actually didn't know he had siblings until he was maybe thirty. We found him after my mother died.

We knew of him, but he didn't know of us. We did some research and I located him and sent him a letter, and, when he called, he said, "I never even knew I had siblings and I always wanted them."

So he came out to visit, and we hit it off immediately—more so than any of the other siblings. When he went back home, we continued to talk almost every day. I felt closer to him than some of the siblings I grew up knowing. We were more like best friends than brother and sister. We told each other everything—however embarrassing it was.

Shawn called me one day and said, "Have you ever heard the song 'I Hope You Dance?'" I said no. At the time, it was playing on country stations and I'm not a country fan. It hadn't crossed over to other radio stations yet. He said, "Look it up and call me back." So I listened to the song and then called him back and said, "Yeah, it's pretty." He asked me if I had listened to all of the words, and I said, "Not really." He told me to listen to the words and then call him back.

I listened to the words and thought, "How interesting is this song? This song is kind of … me." I called Shawn back and said, "It's a great song."

He said, "Can I tell you what it means to me? That is my life in a nutshell. And, if I ever die, that's my song." And I said, "You're not going to die any time soon. And, by the time you die, you'll pick another song." Then he told me he was going through his second round of colon cancer and was not doing well.

He had started a blog called "All It Takes Is Guts." And he talked not just about his cancer story but the funny things he noticed in his treatment and in his recovery. He had this real knack of laughing through the pain. I admired him for it. A lot of people did. He used to post trivial, mundane stuff and make it funny. He would also post this insanely funny stuff about chemotherapy and his hospital stays. He just had a way of making people take notice.

Shawn started running in between chemotherapy sessions. He would run marathons to raise funds for cancer research. He just never stopped living life. Physically, he was half the man. He was not looking well toward the end. He used to play on a softball team, and he had to stop playing, but he would still go to every game and sit on the bench. I started thinking about how he was living his life regardless of his illness. I wrote him an email and said, "Dear Brother, that song is so appropriate. You're dancing."

He died a month later. When he died, I listened to that song again and thought, "What do I do now? How can I dance? What is my dancing?" I never knew that I was going to have to literally dance to answer that question for myself. But I'm dancing now.

Music is the ultimate form of communication.
I think people have been communicating with
each other through music
since the first guy or girl started banging a
stick on a log in a cave a million years ago.

Graham Nash

(Singer/Songwriter)

Music is a conveyor of ideas, and, to me, ideas are the most important form of creation. When I write music, I want to involve people's hearts and their minds, and I want to enable them to sing the melody of what I've written instantly. I'm a very simple songwriter.

I've never believed that people absorb complicated pieces of music quickly. And I want to get their attention now. I want to communicate with as large a pool of people as I can find. That's really what the word "pop" means; it means popular. It means that more people are listening to you.

With the Hollies, we were brilliant at writing two-and-a-half minute songs with a hook that you couldn't forget after you heard it once. We were good at that. We had fifteen or sixteen Top 10 records. After a while, that form of communication started to diminish in my mind. I wanted to write songs that were a little more profound and a little deeper—music that provoked people to not just have a good time and shake their backsides to the music but to also think about what the lyrics meant.

Music to me is all encompassing. My inspiration comes from everything.

I wake up in the morning, look in the mirror, and realize I am still alive and still kicking, and I get on with my day. I'm inspired every day. Without inspiration, I'd be lost.

My day consists of mainly learning what's going on in the world. I'm one of those three-televisions-on with-each-major-channel guys. I want to know everything. And it affects you. I go through all of the emotional changes that every single person I know does. I just happen to be lucky enough to be able to write it down.

The music I write is me being selfish. I'm writing for myself; I don't write for anybody else. It's things I have to say—whether I'm falling in love, or disliking something, or angry at something that went on. I write about what happens to me as a person, and I feel that people can relate to what I write because I am an ordinary person. I am a grounded person; I just happen to do something a little different. I know that I have all these things that I've done in my life, but I'm an ordinary man. I get angry. I fall in love. I get elated.

I'm lucky enough to be able to find melodies that people find hard to forget. I'm an incredibly lucky person. Nobody has to agree with anything I say, but at least give it a listen; you might learn something, because I did when I wrote it. If a song gets past me, I think I stand a good chance of getting it past you because I'm the same as you. Nobody has to agree with what we have to say, but I think we're fortunate enough to have a voice that people sometimes listen to.

I've often thought of interesting melodies and interesting things to say and not had the discipline to write it down, and then I have forgotten them by the next morning. [David] Crosby often says that songs come to him on the edge of sleep, when the elves have taken over the workshop—when your brain is not dealing with what you've dealt with during the day. Your brain relaxes and the elves take over the workshop. That's when David creates a lot. I create a lot then, too.

Whether it's music, painting, collecting, or sculpting, I have to create every day. I have to connect with my kids every day. I'm inspired every day, and I'm grateful for it.

I am always waiting for the elves to come back around the corner.

The power of music stretches way back. In the late '50s and early '60s, it started to change when people like the Weavers and Pete Seeger began to talk about social issues, and then Woody Guthrie and later Bob Dylan. We have always recognized that we're just a link in a giant chain of musicians that stretches back from that guy beating on a log in a cave, all the way through to Lady Gaga today.

I do a lot of things in my life other than music, but music is the driving force. I want people to feel less lonely, less crazy. Maybe somebody else has gone through an experience that they can't quite put into words, and they say, "Oh, I get it. That's what happened to him; that's how he dealt with it."

I don't know where music comes from in my life. People have asked me that question constantly. How do you write music? I have this conveyor belt in my mind that has maybe twenty-four pieces of music being written at the same time. Bits and pieces, and sometimes the inside of my mind will say, "Oh, wait, that line goes with that melody ..."

I can tell whether a song is going to be successful

—both spiritually, in the way it communicates, and commercially, in the way it sells. I know how to write a commercial song; I don't find that difficult at all. I'm the one in our band who has the responsibility of providing those kinds of songs. I think a song can be both commercial and spiritual. Take "Teach Your Children," for instance. I think that's a very spiritual song. I think we have a lot to teach our children, and I think, conversely, we have a lot to learn from our children. But it was an incredibly commercial song.

Radio loved "Teach Your Children." To this day, I hear it played. I got an award from BMI [Broadcast Music, Inc.] several years ago for the couple of million times that "Teach Your Children" was played on the radio. A couple of million times ...

Stephen Stills turned "Teach Your Children" into a hit record because he put that country flavor into it; he was the one who put the B minor in there. When I first played the song for Stephen and David, I'd only lived in America for a couple of months at that point, so, when I sang the song, it kind of sounded like Henry the Eighth doing it. Stephen Stills saved that song.

When I see a fourteen-year-old kid singing "Teach Your Children" today, it's an astounding feeling. Hopefully, the song will outlast this physical body by years and years and years and years.

The first time you kissed anybody, the first time you made love to someone ... Whatever music was playing at that time, if you hear that song later, your mind goes back immediately to that moment. It's very much like a certain smell or a certain taste of food. It has the ability to take you back to the moment that you first loved that music.

People constantly come up and tell me how my music has affected them, and I love that because that's what I'm trying to do. I'm trying to affect people because I'm trying to affect myself. I'm trying to learn. I'm trying to teach. But, most of all, I'm trying to learn and it's a never-ending process. It doesn't show any signs of stopping. I'm in my seventies now, and I'm busier than I've ever been in my life.

It's important to me for people to get juice out of music. It's the same with my photography. I want to use every second of my life to be positive and to move people in a certain direction of thinking about social issues, thinking about romantic songs, thinking about falling in love, thinking about how they deal with things that upset them. Time is our only currency. It's the only thing we have. Even Bill Gates, as rich as he is, can't buy a second of time. My father was dead at forty-six. I'm lucky enough to have had a career in music that stretches over the last fifty years. And I'm still here and I'm still writing.

It took me about twenty-five minutes to write "Just a Song Before I Go." It took me less than an hour to write "Our House." But it took me four years to write "Cathedral" because I was talking about Jesus. I was talking about religion, and I needed to know that every word was in the right place. I had the melody instantly, but the words were something else because I was writing about something that is very important. Religion is very important to a lot of people. It's a form of solace. It's a faith that brings great comfort to many, many people.

I have great faith. I have faith in human beings. I know there are terrible things that go on in the world, but there are also tremendously joyous things that go on in the world and I have faith in this universe. My faith is in the wonderment of dragonflies, of hummingbirds, of flowers, of incredibly beautiful things that happen between human beings. In love and laughter. That's what I have faith in.

And, without hope, there's not much else. We need to feel that tomorrow will be better than today.

We need hope.

Crosby, Stills and Nash did a couple of benefits at my kids' schools, and opening up was this band called Kara's Flowers and they were pretty good. I saw them moving their own amps; I haven't moved my own amp in forty years. I kept looking at this band moving their own drums and stuff, and thought, "Wow. I don't have to do it now, but I did years of that."

A year and a half later, my son Will was at home and I asked whatever happened to Kara's Flowers. He said, "Ah, they're giving up. They're probably going to be doctors and dentists and stuff like that. They've been banging their heads against the wall of the music business and they've given up." And I said, "No. Their music was too good." Even in its raw form. I said, "Here's several thousand dollars; take them back in the studio, have them make demos." That was Maroon 5.

Never give up.

I wrote a line in a song called "Wasted on the Way" which was *"And when you were young did you question all the answers, did you envy all the dancers who had all the nerve?"* I never had the nerve to go up to a lady and ask her to dance. I saw these other kids that were cooler than me who had no problem going up and asking twenty girls to dance. I wasn't one of those people. I'm not a dancer, but I am dancing through this universe. I am dancing through this universe with dignity and laughter, and I do my own kind of dancing. It's not shaking my hips, but I'm dancing.

Promise me that you'll give

faith a fighting chance.

I believe in the powerful connection between the mind, the body, and the spirit. I embrace that we're spiritual beings having human experiences to grow our souls, and I've learned not to judge the challenges.

Suzette Faith-Foster

(Holistic Life Coach, Speaker, and Author)

It was a beautiful fall day in North Carolina, in November 2005. Sunny. Blue sky. The colors in the trees were starting to pop. I love nature. And I loved mountain biking because I was in nature every week, at least once a week. My friend Charlie and I rode our bikes every Thursday morning for a year and a half. This particular day, our friend Andy wanted to join us, so we moved our ride to the afternoon when he could be there. Out on the ride, I could hear the crumble of the leaves underneath the tires, and all of my senses were alive. I wore a camelback hydration system, and it had a pocket for my cell phone. I would always tell Charlie "my cell phone is in the back."

On this particular day, it was the first time I had ever taken my cell phone out of my backpack and showed him my "in case of emergency" (ICE) numbers. Then, we went into the woods. We all love single-track mountain biking. You're leaning into the curbs, and you're going up and over piles of rocks and logs and in and out of gullies. It's exhilarating.

We were biking and had just done our regular "teeter-totter" that's always been on the trail. When you are mountain biking, you go up one side of the trail and the weight of your bike brings you down the other side. We had always done the smaller teeter-totter. We came into the clearing and there was this large teeter-totter, a much higher one with a much thicker board. We looked at it and Charlie moved on. He was going out of town and didn't want to be dealing with that. He was a little more practical than I was.

I had an event that evening, and, energetically, I was preparing my body to succeed. In mountain biking, speed is your friend. I knew I needed to get more speed, so I backed up, and, as I normally do in my spiritual journey, I put the white light around me for protection. I visualized myself on the other side of the teeter-totter—having accomplished it successfully in my mind, and then

I approached the teeter-totter with as much speed as I could get. I got to the top and the next thing I remember is flying over the handlebars.

I knew I was flying through the air and barreling headfirst into the ground. And we heard my head snap. I was instantly paralyzed, and I was lying there on the ground. Charlie ran over to me and I couldn't talk. I mouthed "911" three times. Andy was on the phone calling for help, and Charlie went to get the park ranger. So there I was on the ground. I couldn't move. I couldn't talk. I struggled to breathe.

I had learned to believe and truly embrace that everything has a divine purpose, even something as ugly as what I was going through, and that gave me peace. It allowed me to surrender into the moment and call back my power. I had everything I needed with me because I did have my mind. I'm a spiritual, energetic being that could influence any outcome, and so I had done what I had shared with a lot of my clients to do: I had memorized a mantra to help me get centered again through any big or small life challenge. It came forth the moment I needed it that day.

The mantra I used was:

I refuse to accept this limitation; God is my source.

And, literally, the moment I said that, a lightning bolt-like energy went through my body.

I repeated the mantra:

I refuse to accept this limitation; God is my source.

And, again, instantly, a lightning bolt of energy shot through my body.

This time, my paralyzed hand flopped. It was so much energy that it literally flopped up off the ground. A moment later, I got my breath back. Divine energy and divine healing brought me back to life. So now I'm on the ground totally paralyzed and breathing. I realize later that the Emergency Medical Services (EMS) team took seventeen minutes to get there.

In the ambulance, there was a lot of activity going on, and I chose that opportunity to go within. I knew the healing that I needed. I was going to take everything I knew; everything I had learned to believe; and everything I embraced about the mind, body, and spirit connection. I knew my power was in the power of my mind.

I was peaceful the whole time. I guess what brought me peace was that I'm not afraid of dying. To me, transitioning to the next spiritual realm is going to be so blissful. It's just bliss—love and bliss. So I didn't feel afraid, and I also sensed it wasn't my time. I just sensed a peace about me.

I had chosen a few years ago not to have health insurance. It was a conscious choice. I don't use traditional medicine in most areas of my life. I just said the only reason I would need it would be a horrible accident, and I was naïve enough in my spiritual journey that I didn't think a terrible accident could happen to me. So, of course, I've learned now that things happen not only because of the law of attraction but also because of what our souls are here to experience.

Now I'm lying on the ground and worrying about how I was going to pay the bill. That literally went through my mind. I knew I was going to a hospital, and I was getting a little hard on myself. But I understand that beating yourself up is a lower vibration of energy. I focused that my bill would be paid somehow—and, two months later, money came to pay my hospital bill.

In the ambulance, the EMS team started helping me understand all that I was going through and I realized it didn't sound very pretty. One EMS guy was telling me of his concerns about my broken neck and all the things that were wrong with me. He was doing what he was supposed to be doing—preparing me, helping me understand, helping me to be quiet and still. Yet I knew the power of my mind needed to focus on the positive. I asked him to hold my hand and affirm together that I would be walking. I asked him to see me walking or dancing. He was doing what he needed to do, I was doing what I needed to do, and we became a great team. I asked him to not tell me anything unless it could be positive.

So I started visualizing myself dancing. I love to dance, so I went there in my mind and I blocked out everything they were doing around me. I focused on dancing and that helped me feel peaceful. I ignored where my body was at that moment and instead believed in its power to heal. I knew and believed in the innate power of the body to heal itself, if we give it the right information—and my thoughts were going in that direction of seeing myself dancing.

In the emergency room, there was a lot of commotion—they were doing all of their x-rays and whatever else they were doing. The doctor said that it looked like I had a broken neck, or a severe spinal cord injury, and I thought, "That sounds like it should be serious." I knew where my mind wanted to go, but I wasn't going to give it that much power. My belief system is that the body responds to what you feed it, and I didn't really want to go there.

It wasn't long before family and friends were showing up, and I was reassuring them that this was only a temporary condition—that they should visualize me dancing. I embrace that the universe and our bodies do know what is real and also what we keep telling it energetically with our thoughts and feelings.

When I was in the hospital, I'm sure they all thought

that I was pretty out there. I was saying things about the power of the mind. I know people probably rolled their eyes at me and I'm okay with that, I'm honoring their beliefs and I'm honoring my beliefs. I was seeing myself dancing and here on the x-ray revealed a full quadriplegic. What we have here is a very different approach to healing, to wellness. We have Western traditional medicine, which approaches everything with a basis of Newtonian physics; and then we have mind, body, and spirit, which I see as energy medicine. So we have Newtonian physics with traditional medicine and quantum physics—with mind, body, and spirit, and energy medicine. They are very different.

And there was definitely a difference of opinion in approaching my healing, and, at one point, my doctor got short with me because I was asking him to visualize with me. I think he was genuinely concerned about me, but that wasn't part of his paradigm and he didn't want to go there—I honored that. He made it very clear where he stood, and so there was definitely a difference of opinion, and I honestly didn't care what anyone thought of me.

I got out of surgery at 1:30 in the morning. I realized that they were giving me, or were about to give me, a pain medicine drip, but I refused the pain meds. I believed my body could heal without that pain medicine.

I eat a very consciously healthy diet and I work with the whole body being holistic, so I preferred to not have the chemicals in my body. If I needed them, fine, but I wanted to give my mind power a chance first. I went without pain medications and I did not have any pain. It was the first sign that things were going well with mind power.

The doctors told me I'd be in the intensive care unit (ICU) for seven to ten days. Now that was typical from their experience with totally severed C2 neck vertebra, yet I knew the power of the mind and body, and I just declared, "I'm going to be out of here in two days." And I was out of ICU in two days. I'm sure they thought I was whacky, but I was stating what I wanted, and I was out in those two days.

They told me I'd be in the hospital a minimum of three weeks. I said, "I'll be out in one week." I was literally out in one week. My doctor couldn't quite wrap his head around this phenomenal recovery. He did send me to a rehab hospital. That was his comfort. That was protocol for most people.

So I checked in one afternoon for rehab and, the next morning, they had exercises for me to do and they were evaluating me. By noon, they said, "You don't belong here." I had mobility but I needed to relearn everything. So I went home. The doctor told my friend Jodi not to expect me to get more mobility—that I was a quadriplegic. I was extremely exhausted and tired, and my body needed lots of healing—but I was no longer in the hospital.

When I got home, I was literally in bed for most of three weeks, and, when I was up, I was doing physical therapy. I was walking, but everything was taking every little bit of energy I had. I slept a lot the first three weeks. Or I was in bed doing my meditations and my inner work. When I was up, I had to choose between taking a shower that day and doing my physical therapy. I had very little function in my arms, even though I could move them.

Friends came by, and my mom was there for me. At this point, I could not do anything. I was fully paralyzed. I couldn't button my clothes, I couldn't dress myself, and I couldn't shower. I couldn't dry my hair. I couldn't do the typical things we all take for granted. Even the days when I had showers—that took a lot of my energy, even though someone else was showering me and blow-drying my hair. I had the most amazing angels helping me and taking care of me.

Jodi was my main angel when I broke my neck. As the universe would have it, she had just lost her job the week before. She has a family, but, now, she had more time on her hands to help take care of me. What a blessing that she did that and she did it so amazingly well. She was at my home every day. My friends were all checking my email for me and getting rides organized for doctor appointments. They were all there. Jodi and my friend Amy were sweet to put makeup on me to help me get my look together.

Most of the time, I concentrated on just getting through the day. I had to learn how to button and zip my clothing. I had to learn how to carry a plate and hold things.

My mom was there, doing the meals and basic stuff like laundry. My heart of hearts just thanked her and appreciated everything she did. You're never too old for the healing power of your mother's love and hands. It was very, very hard on her to see me in this condition, and it was hard for her to find her own balance of letting me do a few things and not worrying about me.

She worried a lot, and we had to have a conversation about it because I don't come from a place of worry. One night, she came into the kitchen and I was moving and dancing, and this was probably a couple of days after I got home from the hospital—and she went crazy. I was just moving a little bit, but, to me, it was dancing. I was moving the best I could and that scared her. I had such faith in my innate ability to heal with the mind, body, and spirit. Jodi did, too. She held that energy, but mom didn't have that faith that I had. My other loved ones didn't either, so I can understand why it was scarier for them than it was for me.

Jodi and I are one on our spiritual journey, so she really became my spiritual mentor. We just kept everything positive. It was so wonderful having a friend that could meet me where I was and see everything positive, and we would often laugh. I remember one night my mom was really impatient and wanting my friends to leave because I was getting tired, but I had to say, "Mom, this laughter is healing, too." And it *was* important.

I had come along enough in my spiritual journey to get out of my own way. I could not do a shower. I had to let any of that go. It really wasn't a big deal at the time. I put my big-girl panties on and I did what I needed to do to get my healing going. I had to let any vanity go. It was okay.

A lot changed around the three-week mark. Charlie would come and help me walk three times a week. I would walk a half a mile with his help, and he would just be by my side. On Thanksgiving Day, I walked a mile and a half with a friend, and that was great. A month after my injury, I was walking a mile and a half to two miles every day. I had lost a lot of muscle mass. I had lost a lot of strength. I was relearning everything. I was still doing a lot of physical therapy at home, such as practicing flicking coins and picking things up off the table.

When my friend Andrea came to visit, she brought me this little book with a CD called *I Hope You Dance*. It was based on the song sung by Lee Ann Womack, and, in the front of the book, Andrea wrote "To the day you dance again. I hope you heal quickly." She later told me that she didn't really believe I was going to dance again, but she wanted to give me hope through this book and CD. It really touched me. I had asked everyone to hold that vision of me dancing when we were in the emergency room.

I love to dance. I've always loved to dance. Another friend gave me a plate in my kitchen that says "Dance as if no one's watching." I do dance as if no one's watching. I'm oblivious to what's around and I really go within. I feel joy. And energetic joy is a healing agent in the body. When you feel good, you're sending those good vibrations through your body. So it was wonderful to have the good "I Hope You Dance" vibrations, and it meant a lot to me that Andrea found that book and CD for me.

I've always loved that song. It's just an inspiring, beautiful song. It always made me feel that I'm bigger than my problems. It gave me hope to move through adversity. It came to me at the right time to help me deal with this incredible injury. The song really resonates with what I believe. To hear the song and its uplifting words was just so powerful for me. In my mind, it was the icing on the cake of my already empowering beliefs. I found it important to play it often and to hear it and just stay in that higher vibration.

Some of the lyrics really speak to me. *"I hope you never lose your sense of wonder."* I know I have sometimes gotten too close to taking things for granted. This is an incredible universe, and I like being reminded of that. *"You get your fill to eat but always keep that hunger."* I equate that spiritually. No matter what I do on a spiritual level, no matter what I'm being thankful for, no matter how much I deepen my faith, I really want to keep that hunger.

"Promise me that you'll give faith a fighting chance" is a powerful lyric for me. I see that everything I do comes from the opportunity to look at it a certain way, and, if I didn't have faith, I would be trying to control the outcome or I would be so worried because I didn't know what the outcome would be. But faith gives me the chance to settle in and relax into the problem, knowing that a higher power is at work. In my world, faith is what moves us through our obstacles. Faith is what helps us push our foot forward when everything else just feels so down and so wrong.

I'm a living testament of *"may you never take a breath for granted."* That speaks to me now more than ever. Life can change in a split second, and the accident has helped me live more fully every day, and it has helped me embrace the quiet times, or what we might have called the boring times. Everything is perfect. Everything is okay because everything has a purpose. It's part of the puzzle. I know I have gotten too close to tragedy to take things for granted.

"Give the heavens above more than just a passing glance" speaks to me, embracing my spiritual journey. Everything is about our spiritual journey—we're here to grow our soul. If I focus too much on the here and now, life can get at me—but when I give the heavens more than a passing glance, it reminds me that, when I rise about the chaos that I'm observing, it just totally transmutes the energy. It brings me into another place of surrendering to what *is*, and when I surrender to what is the universe, my spirit starts to orchestrate resolutions that I could never have thought of. So I love that lyric.

At the time of my accident, my daughter Brittany was a senior in high school. She and her sister had been living with their dad for two and a half years. They went to live there because of our dynamics. It was a very challenging relationship. Teenage daughters can go through quite a challenge, and Brittany was dealing with anger issues and some depression, and she had not wanted to get any help for it. Even when we coerced her into getting help, she really wasn't engaging the way she could have in order to get better.

So we were dealing with this challenging situation

with her and I was into my spiritual journey. I was into my energy healing some at that time, and, as a mom, it was heartache for me to see Brittany suffer and not want my help. But I believe my children are my teachers. I believe that everyone around me is a teacher. I had to ask myself, "What can I learn from her?" I had to learn boundaries. I had to learn self-love and self-respect because I was not getting it from her at all.

And I did what was the hardest thing I had ever done in my life up to that point. When Brittany was a sophomore in high school, I had to kick her out of the house. She wouldn't get help. She was deeply and excruciatingly angry. She hated the world and I got that projected onto me. It wasn't every second of every day, but it was often. Brittany wouldn't respect my rules, and she wouldn't go to counseling. I had to learn tough love, and that's not fun either.

I knew I wasn't going to enable her, and I knew that if I didn't lay down strong rules that I *was* enabling her. That didn't feel good to me at all. I wanted to parent her. I really wanted her to go to therapeutic boarding school when she was a sophomore, but her dad wouldn't go for that. He ended up deciding that he would take both of the girls.

And what I was hoping would be six months with her dad ended up being the rest of high school for her—

two and a half years. It was really hard for me because it was very challenging when we did see each other. Her dad originally thought it was mother-daughter dynamics, and he thought it was a problem for us to work out. But he found out very quickly when Brittany moved in with him that she was in a place where she didn't want to look at herself. She didn't want to take responsibility for her actions. She was very volatile and impulsive, and it was a very challenging time.

At the time of my injury, Brittany was very loving and caring when it first happened. I don't know if she really understood how to handle it because she had not learned how to process her feelings in a healthy way. She went home the night of the surgery and painted. I had told her a while before that, if I ever got a tattoo, it would be a heart with wings. So, when I was in ICU, she brought me a painting of a heart with wings. The wings had yet to dry. I couldn't talk. I had a breathing tube down my throat. But I could feel her love, I could feel her caring. I knew she was worried, and I felt that it was positive that she had channeled her feelings into the painting. I couldn't talk to her, I couldn't comfort her, but I knew we had a love there and I felt that love.

This gives me deep faith in humanity, because we are here to grow through challenges. It gives me great faith in my daughter. I believe in Brittany. I know she's going to rock this world one day when she figures out how to do it on her terms.

I love the line in the song that says, *"I hope you never fear those mountains in the distance."* When I start seeing life from a higher perspective, it's what I came here to learn about and to work and move through.

My relationship with Brittany is still a work in progress. We are still learning to honor each other's opinions and different viewpoints. As we start to heal our inner hurts, the shine happens.

Today, I am fully functioning. I'm not completely healed. The remnants I have are some numbness in my fingertips, and a little bit of numbness throughout my body. I still have a stiff neck and a spinal cord injury. Any fall I have can stretch the scar tissue and cause me to have a setback in my paralysis—a little or a lot, depending on the injury. I listen to my gut if I'm to do anything. I do mountain biking on a flat surface, and I listen to myself. *"Living might mean taking chances but they're worth taking"* resonates with me. I don't want to live in a shell now that I've had my injury. I choose not to snow ski anymore. I loved to snow ski, but I know what feels right and what doesn't. It does feel right to get back on the bike, and it feels right to rollerblade.

When I was in the hospital, I knew that my mind would get me well. I had to ignore what was so painfully obvious to everyone else, that I was quadriplegic. And, because of that, I am alive today and fully functioning. I needed to go through this injury for my destiny path's highest good. Life's challenges have a purpose. We consciously may not want them, but on a spiritual journey, it's exactly what our soul needed to go to its next level of consciousness.

I believe our souls are here to expand in consciousness. We're humanity. We're here to expand our faith to a higher power. I think most of us would agree that, when we look back over our challenges, most of us could say, "Wow, I didn't like it at the time, but I grew a lot from that."

I should have been dead. I should have been a quadriplegic. I am living proof that the mind can create positive change. That we can rise above any challenge. That we can look at our challenges in a different way. I am living proof that we are more than what meets the eye.

"When you get a choice to sit it out or dance ..." That line just has such beautiful meaning to me.

I still get to practice to choose to dance every day.

And I choose to dance.

I choose to dance.

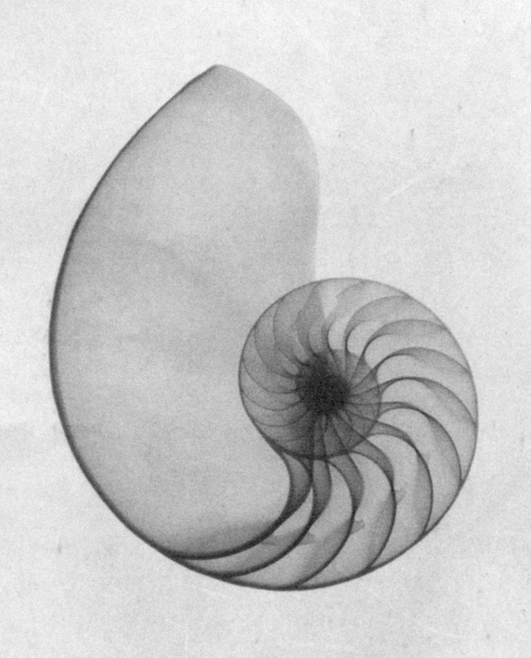

Music is what makes me tick.
It's what makes me want to breathe.
It's so deep seated in me
that I can't fathom life without it.

Vince Gill

(Singer/Songwriter)

I had an older brother and an older sister, and my parents and everybody were music nuts. The whole family loved music. My first conscious memory of ever hearing anything was a hymn called "How Great Thou Art." I heard my grandma play it on a piano. I still have a foggy memory of sitting on the piano bench with her on weekends, hearing her play that. I listened to the radio all the time because I was trying to learn to play—so I tried to learn anything and everything I could hear. The first record I ever bought with my own money was either "Twist and Shout" by the Beatles or the Jerry

Napoleon XIV novelty hit song "They're Coming to Take Me Away, Ha Haaa." So that would explain the madness in my brain. I still have all those records, and that's pretty neat. In a day where music has become somewhat disposable, I have something that I've had for fifty years. I didn't pay much for it, but it sure lasted me a long time. I value music a whole lot more than the world does for what they charge for it.

If you go throughout history, there were many lame records made in the '50s, and there were just as many lame records made in the '60s. Every era had lame records made. But that's why you remember the great ones. We're all hoping to move the meter in some way—even if we move the meter in fun. A lot of songs out there today just crack me up. But they're moving the meter for somebody. I think songs can be about anything and can touch people in any number of ways, but what I miss are great melodies. Go listen to a Roy Orbison record, and you'll hear some great melodies. "Somewhere Over the Rainbow" is one of the most beautiful melodies ever written. There's still some great stuff going on today.

I've personally always been drawn to the more melancholy side of music. Happy music never did much for me. It made me want to change the channel. I wanted to hear the angst and I wanted to hear the blue side. I wanted to hear the drama. I think, for a lot of people, deep down there is a melancholy, and music seems to do something to soothe that. Millions of people can like a hit song, but, at the end of the day, it's something that floats out in the air and you just respond to it. Everybody's different, but we're all the same, too.

As a songwriter, to create and record a song that actually does something powerful for people is the greatest feeling you could ever hope to have—that you helped people out during their hardest times. I have one song, "Go Rest High On That Mountain," and it's a song I wrote when my brother passed away. I wasn't even going to record it. My goal was to honor my brother with what I thought was in store for him and what I'd hoped for him and believed for him. Believe it or not, it's become probably the most performed song at funerals—even rivaling "Amazing Grace," they tell me. It's great to know that you can comfort people with your music.

Reacting to success is easy, but, when life is at its darkest and you're struggling hard, that's when you really identify your character. That's when you really see what you're made of.

I'm married to a woman, Amy [Grant], whose music has really brought people to faith, which has changed lives. It's pretty astounding to see how many lives she's impacted with her music because of what it says. To me, music is more than coming up with a clever idea and having a three-minute hit. I want to be moved.

I'm moved by music, so, in turn, I don't want to become rich by making music. I want to move people with my music. That will never change. I can play a million shows and, if people don't respond, it breaks your heart. If you're playing and they don't respond, it's like a conversation that is going nowhere. During concerts, if we're talking to each other, then that's a great feeling. But, when the conversation is one way and nothing comes back from the audience, it's pretty tough to stomach some nights.

I think it's interesting that, in the thirty-five or more years that I've been in the studio, the great songs have come the easiest. Some songs come easy. Great songs play themselves, in a sense. It's just so simple when the puzzle is put together for you. All you do is get out of the way and enhance a great song. The ones you labor over and struggle with sometimes, they're not the best songs.

Some songs that I thought would be the most successful haven't been. I've been fooled many, many times. The real exercise is to find something that's honest and real, and then people will respond to it. I think people can spot the phony, the fake, the posing. Entertainers like the Beatles and James Taylor are what make us get better. They inspire us to be better. I take a lot of comfort in knowing that there are so many people out there who still move the meter for me.

My definition of success is analyzing if I'm getting better. And I am. I feel like I am, and that, to me, is all I can do. I'm not as popular as I once was, with hit records and being in your face all the time. But I'm so much better than I was then. I have never had control over the success or the failure of my music. I never believed all the good things people said about me, and I never believed the bad things they said about me. I just tried to ride right down the middle.

I had the "I Hope You Dance" kind of success with "When I Call Your Name." People were rooting for me to succeed and, when I finally broke through and had that career record, everybody went "yay, finally."

"I Hope You Dance"—that record, that song, that artist, that production—everything about it was perfect. It was perfect timing. And I think it will be Lee Ann's definitive career song.

I have written songs with both Mark and Tia over the last 25 years, and I say "yay" for them, too. They really hooked a big one. It really is a song of hope—of wishing the absolute best for somebody. It doesn't get better than that.

"I Hope You Dance" was a crossover record. A great song doesn't have to sit in a certain genre of music. I don't know what it is about certain songs that speak to people like they do, but that one sure did. It has great lyrics, and there are certain records like that throughout history. It was the perfect song. When those things line up, you just get out of the way because it's awesome to watch. Lee Ann hooked it and she knocked it out of the park. At that time, there weren't many traditional country singers like her. A lot of people who really revere and love the traditional side of this music really championed her and rooted for her and supported her. Being one of them, I was so thrilled.

I think what's so great about the song is that it doesn't just pigeonhole you in one stretch of time. There's nothing worse than "me, me, me" in a song. A song that's all about self is not interesting to me. A song like "I Hope You Dance" only comes along every once in a while, and that makes it even more special to me. I'm glad they're not all that good.

"I Hope You Dance" is a loving song, and I like that it relates to any relationship or to any part of our lives.

I think hope and faith are similar. Having faith in something is a lot about hope. It's mean out there. There are ugly people, there are mean people, and there are people who struggle mightily.

And if you don't have hope, what's the point? Hope is the big word in the big show here today. I'm grateful that I have optimism and belief in something better that's going to happen and that is worth making the effort for.

Whenever one door closes

I hope one more opens.

Once we move into whatever
you believe is the next life,
you don't really need your organs
and there is the opportunity
to bestow life upon others

Bill Thomasson

(Parent of Teenage Organ Donor)

I was born in a small town in the southern part of Virginia, a little town called Martinsville, which was quite a bit different from where I find myself today in the big city. It was a small town where the primary industries were knitting plants. At one point, the town was called the "Sweatshirt Capital of the World" and the "Furniture Capital of the World."

The best thing about a small town is also the worst thing about a small town—which is that everybody knows everybody. When my brother and I were growing up, there was nothing we could get away with. If we did anything that we shouldn't have been doing, our father would know about it before we saw him next.

I met Taylor's mother, Pat, at Virginia Tech. When we both completed our degrees, we were looking for opportunities in a larger metropolitan area, and the Washington, D.C., area provided the best opportunities for both of us.

We had some challenges trying to conceive a baby, but, with some medical assistance, we were excited to finally be expecting our first child. Taylor came into our life in March of 1989. She was the joy of my life from the first day. I was in the delivery room when Taylor was delivered.

Pat had to go through a cesarean section to deliver Taylor. When she was in the recovery room her blood pressure started dropping and we got a bit of a scare. They had to go back in and as it turned out the doctor had nicked Pat's spleen. So she had to go back to the operating room for that. I was concerned about her but was assured she was okay. It turned out to be a moment I will never forget. I was able to go into the nursery and give Taylor her first bottle. It was indescribable. There was no greater experience that I could have had.

Taylor was the light of my eye and continues to be.

Taylor was very active in her early years. She started school at the age of two and a half. Her self-awareness was acute, so Taylor jumpstarted her education at the local Montessori school. We soon found out in her first parent-teacher conference that she tended to be a little bored by the classroom. Unfortunately, on a number of occasions, she wound up in the head mistress's office. The headmistress and Taylor's teacher soon figured out that that wasn't punishment for Taylor. She *wanted* to be with the adults. She was bored being with her peers.

That was good news/bad news because it was obvious that Taylor was advanced over her years. It also created some challenges with her in terms of social interaction. I think she was a bit introverted.

In elementary school, Taylor participated in a unique Japanese immersion program for three years. The first half of her day, she received her instruction in English and the second half of the day it was in Japanese. She picked up Japanese again in high school. That was one of the common interests for her and her friends, the "Thank Goodness It's Friday Ladies." Each of the TGIF Ladies tended to not only share a common bond in terms of interest—Japanese, in particular, but also the arts.

One of the reasons she selected Penn State as her college was her interest in perhaps continuing her study of Japanese. Taylor's mother was born in Germany. Pat's father, who was in the Air Force, later moved the family to Tokyo. Pat had shared her experiences with Taylor, so Taylor gravitated toward that.

Taylor's mother and I separated when Taylor was six. Originally, we agreed upon shared custody. A few months after we separated, Taylor's mother decided to relocate to Portland, Oregon. At that point, we agreed that Taylor would live with me during the school year and then she would be with her mother during the Christmas holidays, spring break, and summer.

I missed Taylor every summer, but I knew she was with her mother and was safe.

I would travel to visit Taylor and spend time with her in the Oregon area. We did a lot of exploration. Oregon and Washington have the largest percentage of national parks in any two states in the U.S., and one of Taylor's favorite spots outside of the Portland area was Multnomah Falls.

Later on, that had some significance, in that her English teacher, Mr. Butterfield, had a picture of Multnomah Falls in his classroom. When I first met Mr. Butterfield, who was one of Taylor's favorite teachers, he said that the photo of Multnomah Falls was the first conversation starter between him and Taylor. He had felt that she was a little bit shy and introverted, but her interest in the photo brought her out of her shyness.

The separation was tough for Taylor. She did act out a bit, and those first years were rather challenging. For most parents, the more difficult years are the teen years. For me, what I found in the middle years were the most difficult. We actually went through some therapy sessions with her. Once Taylor got to high school, she got into a circle of friends (her TGIF Ladies) that she was comfortable with, and she felt accepted by them.

Sometimes some people don't fit into the mainstream. Taylor didn't appreciate people for their clothes or their money; she appreciated them for the time they spent with her. Those are not my words; those are the words that my brother shared about her in his eulogy at her funeral.

Taylor and I did spend time together in high school. I think we had a great relationship. We were open with each other, and I never really felt that Taylor was unwilling to share things with me. We did do a lot of things together. She would share her experiences. In the evenings, we often watched television or movies together. One of the great things about living in the D.C. area is that we have a lot of history around and Taylor was a big history buff. She had an almost encyclopedic knowledge of the First Ladies. One of her favorite exhibits down downtown was the Smithsonian exhibit on the First Ladies. She had some strong opinions about politics and politicians and other things related to the presidency.

Taylor considered different universities, but she had some great recommendations for Penn State and she was accepted there right away. Her verbal skills were exceptional; she had scored 780 out of 800 on her verbal SATs. She wasn't by any means a merit scholar, but her SAT scores plus her academic record meant that she graduated summa cum laude from her high school.

Like any parent, I had mixed emotions about her going off to college. I was concerned about the size of the school. The campus is roughly 40,000 students, so I talked to Taylor about that. Her pushback was that she was attending the largest high school in Virginia. I suggested to her that she might want to consider a different dorm choice because one of the options they offered was a dorm where you could participate as a group, a more cohesive type of group.

I knew from my own college experience that those first days can be difficult—the pull from home to a new place and making friends. In Taylor's early days at Penn State, her mother and I spoke with her every day. I went up on a number of occasions to visit her. One of our favorite spots of campus was in the commons area at a student hangout called The Big Onion. I can remember getting our grinder sandwiches there. We had good times when I went up to visit her there. There is a tree, a plaque, and a bench on campus now, in her memory.

Taylor had a difficult time keeping roommates. She and her first roommate weren't able to come to an agreement on something. The roommate wanted her boyfriend to sleep over and Taylor wasn't comfortable with that. The roommate eventually moved out, and there was a period of time when Taylor did not have a roommate.

We were excited when Taylor said that she had a new roommate, and we hoped it would work out. Unfortunately, it didn't. The roommate lasted a week or so. I talked with Taylor about it, and her mother had had a similar experience in her original college days, so she could be more empathic. Taylor indicated that everything was fine. But, later in the semester, something caused her to become even more introverted. She reassured her mother and me, saying that she was fine having her dorm room to herself. She liked the privacy.

Taylor was a little bit of out of sync with her peers. She was excited because she had made two friends in the hall there, but that also turned out to be a bittersweet thing in that both of them decided that they were going to be dropping out of Penn State at the end of the semester to go to a different university.

I asked a counselor in the housing office to follow up with Taylor. The counselor told me that she had talked with Taylor and that Taylor was comfortable and everything was okay. But things weren't okay, and that led up to a call I received one morning, indicating that Taylor had been found outside of her dorm, unconscious.

It was very surreal. The call was from the vice president of student affairs. He said that Taylor was being transferred from the campus hospital to the regional trauma center in Altoona, Pennsylvania, about an hour away. I was advised to get there as soon as I could.

On my way up there, I periodically checked in with the hospital chaplain. I knew that the prognosis was not good because, as I was on the way, he asked me about my feelings about saying last rites for Taylor. That just dried my throat.

I made it to the hospital in record time. There, I met the hospital chaplain and the representative from Penn State. They couldn't really tell me a whole lot more. The Penn State representative said that it seemed Taylor had taken a fall or had jumped from her dorm room window, eight stories up. It was just incredulous to believe that. A detective with the campus police told me that their investigation was continuing, but, at this point, they had found no signs of foul play.

The worst words a parent can hear is, "There's nothing more we can do." I can also understand, from a medical profession standpoint, that those are words they never want to say to a parent. I feel very strongly that there's always something you can do. You can give more. And given Taylor's generosity and caring for others, I viewed the opportunity to donate Taylor's organs—and not only organs but also her tissue, as an opportunity to see her live on through others.

I had spoken with Taylor on the phone the night before she died. There was nothing unusual about our conversation. "Everything is fine," she said. "I'm doing well."

I think we talked about her classes, and she had mentioned that there was a frustration about class changes and the rush to get across campus to her classes, which was a bit of a challenge. We ended our call as we usually did. I love you. I miss you.

A couple weekends prior, she had begged me to come up and take her home again. Obviously, I had wanted to see her, and, as it turned out, it was also the last opportunity for her to spend with the TGIF Ladies. I think that had some significance because I will never forget that, when I picked her up, she grabbed me in a bear hug and I think this was something she had planned out in her mind. We all know hindsight is 20/20, but, after the fact, it did have some significance and it all started to fit together.

Given the distance from Oregon, Pat didn't arrive until the following morning. We went up to the trauma area and that was the first time we saw Taylor. It was just total disbelief. Taylor was nonresponsive. I was feeling shell-shocked. The first thing I noticed was that her leg was in a splint. Tubes and instruments were all around her. She had a collar on her neck. Her eyes were partially open but kind of rolled back. It was devastating to see our bright, lively daughter like this. It was just heartbreaking.

I was in a bit of denial about the seriousness of the situation. Pat and I insisted that the doctors prove to us that there was no hope for her to recover. We were shown a graph of Taylor's brainwave activity in comparison to that of normal brainwave activity, and Taylor's was pretty flat in comparison.

When we removed her respirator, we still hoped against all hope that she would start to at least show some indication that she was trying to breathe on her own. But there was no response. That was pretty much the final confirmation, and we had to accept the fact that the Taylor we knew and loved was gone.

We knew that Taylor supported organ donation, so we made the decision to donate her organs.

The final goodbye was tough. In my wildest dreams, I could never have imagined an end like that. No one wants to give up their child. But that was the reality of life. We had recognized that Taylor's time had come for her to go on, but it didn't make it any easier to accept it. Looking back, there was that glimmer of hope for the future; we know she had made the world a better place for having been here.

After Taylor's death, Pat and I went to Penn State to gather her belongings. We saw the very buses that should have been bringing Taylor home for Thanksgiving. Outside of her dorm area, we saw the place where her body had fallen. We went up to her room and everything was spic and span. She had done all of her laundry. Everything was in perfect order. Clothes and everything laid out. The detective told us that, upon entering the room, he found her laptop and there was a playlist of songs that was still playing. Taylor had a playlist of ten songs, and one of the songs that was playing was "I Hope You Dance."

It's the paradox that I deal with.

The other lyric that jumps out at me is *"when one door closes, another one opens."* I think that's true with Taylor and our decision to donate her organs. In this case, a door closed for me in terms of my life with my daughter, but yet another door has opened. Many doors have opened. Like her good friends who have come in to support me.

Pat and I made the decision to put lyrics from "I Hope You Dance" on her gravestone. It seemed to us to epitomize Taylor and what we would want others to think about when they visited her grave site. We also added her name in Japanese because that was important to her. Another thing on her gravestone was inspired by a mural at the spiritual center at Penn State that depicts a shepherd gathering his flock. We couldn't put the entire expanse on her gravestone, but we included certain elements of it.

Faith has given me solace that Taylor is now whole. She's no longer in pain, the mental pain of anguish that she experienced, so that gives me solace. What gives me further solace is that she is living on through others.

I take pride in the accomplishments of her friends, and I take great solace in the support they continue to provide me. They're my adopted daughters. They're busy and active doing other things now, but they continue to support me in any way they can and I'm greatly appreciative. And I think it's indicative of the friendships and bonds that Taylor had formed with them.

I drafted a letter to each of the organ recipients, indicating that Pat and I had waived the confidentiality and that we would like for them to do likewise if they were comfortable with us meeting them and getting to know them. All but two of Taylor's recipients responded favorably.

There is so much that can be done with organ donations, so much good. There are more than 100,000 people on any given day that are on the waiting list for organs. I became an organ donor. I have to admit I was not an organ donor before Taylor's death, but I am now.

Several years ago, when I was making a message to promote organ donation, I was asked, "If Taylor were sitting here with us today, what would she say?" And no doubt in my mind, she would have said, "I hope you dance."

That was Taylor. She loved her friends, she loved her family, and I know without a doubt that she is looking down on her organ recipients because she knows they are living for her. I have no doubt that she would be dancing.

In memory of Taylor, Pat and I started an "I Hope You Dance" team for a local Donate Life Run/Walk event. We have a purpose in life, and, once that purpose has been met, we have to move on and we have to accept that.

Her heart recipient was able to see his granddaughter. Her cornea recipient was able to continue on with her family and to do the things that she hadn't been able to do. And her kidney recipient was able to go from three dialysis treatments per week to none. He is ecstatic over that. He is able to dance now that he's untethered from dialysis.

It's the idea of the life cycle going on. There's not a day that goes by that I don't miss Taylor. We all do. I would love for her to be with us. We have the memories, but organ donation is an opportunity for new memories and new things to happen.

In her early years, Taylor would always have to do a performance when we would have company over for dinner.

She would dance for the audience.

Oh, how she would dance.

After darkness, light

I never really thought about music helping people until I became a recording artist. I have to be careful what I say in music because people take this really literally and very seriously. Depending on what they're going through in their lives, your song may come on the radio and it may be an epiphany for that person at that moment.

Lee Ann Womack

(Singer/Songwriter)

I remember just falling in love with Glen Campbell when I was a little girl. "By the Time I Get to Phoenix." "Galveston." "Wichita Lineman." All those songs really struck a chord with me. His voice was just so pretty, along with the string arrangements, those Jimmy Webb songs, and the melodies. It all fit together really well, and that made a big impression on me as a small child.

I don't remember a time in my life when I didn't want to be a singer. I was little when I first saw Dolly Parton on TV, and I wondered then how she got to be on television. I remember thinking that I might like to do that someday, too. Music is the soundtrack of our lives. Music makes people act differently, and it really moves people to do things.

There's nothing like feeling connected to the listeners when they come to you after a show and tell you a story about how your song affected them. They'll tell you when they heard it, and when they bought it and played it for people. How they listen to it every day before they go to work. I love it when people have a story they can tell me. For musicians, that's when you think that maybe what you do is not just entertainment—maybe it really does help people sometimes.

After I cut "I Hope You Dance," a lot of people would come to my meet-and-greet events (which were always right before the show) and they would tell me stories and a lot of them were really hard, difficult, sad stories—a lot of them involving children. I'm just crazy about kids, and these stories would be so powerful and would affect me so much that I wouldn't able to go on and sing a 90-minute concert effectively and do my job really well. So I had to move the meet-and-greet sessions to after the show.

I have people stop me in the grocery store to this day and tell me how "I Hope You Dance" has affected them and their lives. They're very personal stories and they have made me think about a lot of things that I had not thought of before. But I'm not a counselor—I'm just a country singer from East Texas. These stories, though, have helped me to grow as a person and have helped me relate to people in new ways.

I'm thankful for that, actually. I make music for a living. It's what I do. My husband does, too. We're always writing and looking for other artists, other new writers, looking for new songs to record.

I remember Mark Wright calling me and saying, "Get down here right now, you've got to hear this song." He played it for me, and it made me think of my daughters, Aubrie Lee and Anna Lise, and all the things I wanted for them in their life. I didn't think about anything else except that this is what I want for my daughters. I found a personal point in the song and then decided to cut it for that reason. I didn't think about it possibly being a hit. I just thought, "Let's cut this; it reminds me of my kids." It's about picking yourself up, having hope, letting moments pass you by. This song really does have a lot of meaning in a lot of different ways and, as the artist, you can start putting all those things together.

All songs are special in one way or another or else you wouldn't cut them. We cut several things the day we cut "I Hope You Dance" and, at the time, it didn't particularly stand out above the other ones. I remember

Ricky Skaggs was coming in to sing on that record and I was all fired up about another cut on that record.

All songs have their special qualities and, when you're right in the middle of making the record, you're thinking of overdubs, you're thinking of who's going to play guitar on this or who's going to sing harmony on that. I do remember thinking that "I Hope You Dance" was going to be a single that I'd like to include my girls on. It was very innocent and honest on my part. It was just personal to me, and I want people to see what the song means to me.

The first time I heard the demo, it made me think about my children and all the things I wanted for them. The most life-changing moment for me, as far as the song goes, was that first listen, because, from then on, I thought about my girls every single time I heard it.

I had had a couple of No. 1 hits before that and had sold a lot of records. I was just rolling along and, at the time, this song was actually just another country song that I had recorded. Nothing really stood out to me until I got a call from my best friend back home in East Texas, and she said, "I swear I was driving down the road and heard 'I Hope You Dance' on the *pop* station."

I called Mark Wright and told him about my friend hearing it on a Top 40 station, and he said, "Yeah, we're throwing it out there; we're testing it a little bit. We'll see if it's going to work."

Soon the song was playing on Top 40 stations. I was so busy that I still didn't have time to think about it much. I loved the song and I kept thinking about what it meant to me and especially for my children. At some point, I began to think about what it meant for everybody else's children, too

With "I Hope You Dance," a lot of things had to line up right for so many people to hear that song. There are some great songs that artists have recorded that don't get a lot of the chances that "I Hope you Dance" did, but, fortunately, everything lined up right. One person told another and another told another, and it just snowballed. I got lucky with "I Hope You Dance." I'm very lucky.

It probably wasn't the smartest thing in the world, putting my kids in the music videos. I just didn't think about it. I was thinking that my parents would love to see them in the videos. The baby couldn't walk when we started planning the video and they wanted her running around, but she was a late walker, so we didn't know if she was going to be walking in time. She started letting go of the coffee table and taking a couple of steps—and that was as much as she had done. On the day that we made the video, we just let go of her and she just started running around. It was awesome. She did a great job and was trying to dance. She was watching me and trying to mimic some of the things I was doing. She stole the show on the video.

When you're the child of an artist, your parent's business is all so common-place for them. My children don't really listen to my music. They know all the songs and everything, but they're not impressed. They don't really have any "I Hope You Dance" stories or anything like that. I think they probably just roll their eyes at this point. Their life is so different than mine. I can look at them and see that they're totally not impressed by what mom does.

My daughters both have dreams and aspirations of their own. I work really hard to make sure that, if they are a round peg, they're not trying to fit into a square hole. I won't let anybody else do that to them, either. I know what it was like growing up being different. I would tell people as a kid that I was going to go to Nashville and be a country singer, and they all thought I would grow out of it by high school. I was still saying it then, though, and I think they were feeling sorry for me by that time. I just don't want my girls to be in that situation. If they think they want to be an astronaut or whatever they want to be, that'd be great. I hope that I've been able to provide that kind of environment for them. I was able to run off and chase my dreams, and I just want to make sure that they're able to do that, too, and that they feel like they can.

I remember looking at Oprah when she had the "I Hope You Dance" CD in her hand. She was clutching it and singing every word along with me, and I just thought, "Wow." I never in a million years would have dreamed that I would be there, with Oprah singing my song back to me. She was so happy about it, and you could tell that she really, really loved it—and that meant a lot to me. That's what I remember most about my performance on her show.

I don't really watch much TV, but, when somebody sings "I Hope You Dance," my phone blows up. Most people watch *American Idol* and they know all the contestants, and they'll say "Susan's singing your song"—or whoever's on. So I will get lots of messages about it being performed. Or if they play it at some other event, people will call me. I don't usually hear it firsthand, but I usually hear about it.

I know how lucky I am. Not everybody gets to have a dream their whole life and then have the opportunity to go and pursue that dream—and then it comes true and you get to do what you love for a living. Not everybody gets to do that, and I am so thankful because music is my life.

What's so great about "I Hope You Dance" is that it doesn't have a story, so every listener is able to put their own story into it. I think that's one of the reasons that the song has touched so many people. In the grand scheme of things, "I Hope You Dance" is just another song. But it has really changed a lot of people and a lot of things.

There are a lot of people who know "I Hope You Dance" but don't know any of the rest of my music. I was a traditional country artist from deep East Texas. My dad was into country radio. Country music is what I live for, professionally speaking. I'm passionate about real hardcore, traditional country music. But there are a lot of people who know "I Hope You Dance," and they'll come to the show. They want to hear it. That's the song they came for, so we do it in every show. I never sing it the same way twice, much to the chagrin of my band members, who have to be on their toes at all times. I don't ever plan, and I never know what's going to come out of my mouth when I open it.

When I perform "I Hope You Dance" live, people will bring a slip of paper or whatever and say "It's my birthday. Can you dedicate 'I Hope You Dance' to me?" And, usually, somebody will be there with sign that says something like, "We danced to this at my son's wedding."

It's hard to dance if you're not a dancer, to put yourself out there, whether it be literally on a dance floor or just in life and to take those chances. When I think of dancing, it's "go ahead and dance like nobody's watching you—live life to the fullest."

I hope that, if my daughters get the chance to sit it out or dance, that they do take the chance and dance.

Loving might be a mistake,

but it's worth making.

It's hard to forgive yourself
and the mistakes you made
when you were younger
when you realize that you're not a different person.
I'm not a different person, just a more mature person.
It's okay to hold on to experiences you've had because,
ultimately, they make you a better person.
It sounds cliché, and everybody says it,
but it's the truth.

Stephanie Willoughby

(Television Producer, Reluctant Bride)

I was born in Michigan and then my dad was transferred to Chicago, so I grew up in the western suburbs of Illinois. I attended Catholic school from kindergarten through 12th grade. I've always been a very obedient girl. I'd love to be one of those Catholic school girls who rolled my skirt, smoked cigarettes, and intentionally flirted with older men, but I was never really one of those people.

I did what I was told and never missed curfew. And if I did, I called. I had a great group of friends—the same girls that I'm still friends with now. I was just a really adventurous little girl, but not a difficult child. My parents may tell you something different. But I feel like I'd love to have gotten me as a kid. I was easy—a really easy, easy-going good Catholic girl. I really was.

When I was younger, I definitely wanted to be a dancer, a rock star, an actress. And then I quickly learned that I was not talented. So that was a problem. You need to be talented to do those things. And I don't have the type of parents who would say, "You can do anything." They're very business minded and very much "You actually *can't* sing, so that's probably out for you. You play no instruments despite three years of piano lessons." I still can't play "Chopsticks."

So, as I got a little bit older, I wanted to be a newscaster. For a while, I wanted to be like Barbara Walters. But then I realized that being a newscaster required a lot more work than I was willing to do. I'm not the type to go to Hong Kong and talk about communists. It's just not me. I wouldn't do well in those kinds of environments, so that was out.

And then I really loved crafting when I was in high school. I had this door in my bedroom, a white door and it was paneled. I would take photos I had with myself and my friends and things out of magazines, words and letters. I would hot-glue them to the back of my door and make giant collages.

And, because I felt I was really talented at making these collages, I would make small collages for all my friends. Then my friends and I would exchange collages. This was my thing. But you can't be a professional collage maker. You can't really go to school for that. So, ultimately, my mother decided that I was going to be a producer—even though she didn't know what a producer did. But it made sense since it was a lot about storytelling and I had that collage skill, so that was good. That's how my family is—we'll just tell you what you're going to do and eventually we'll say it so often you'll just do it.

But it worked out and I have really enjoyed my career choice. The bottom line was that my mom was right. I ultimately produced television segments and then started editing them.

I definitely wanted to get married and have children. I wanted more of a storybook life. My mom always worked my whole life. As an adult, I don't know how she did it. I remember wanting her to be homeroom mom and to go on field trips. I begged her to do all those things, but she wasn't able to because she worked. Back in the 1980s, a lot of moms didn't work. But the mom of my childhood best friend also worked, so when my friend and I would play together, we would pretend we were at meetings. We had very important meetings and we had clients. We had all these catch phrases. And other kids were saying,

"I just want to have kids. What are you guys doing?" So we said, "We're going to grow up and we're going to go to meetings and we're going to be so powerful ..."

But, in truth, I really didn't want to be so powerful. I didn't really want to go to meetings. I wanted to stay home with my kids because I wanted to be homeroom mom. I wanted to do it to the 100th degree and be awesome at it. But I didn't think as much about the wife part.

When I was in high school, the perfect guy for me just had to be cute and athletic. I wasn't so worried about financial success or any type of success. I was more concerned with popularity. I was head of the Pom Poms, which was the dance team. So I intentionally dated whoever was really doing well at sports at the time.

By the time I got to college, I was looking for someone who could navigate New York. I moved there and went to NYU. When I left for college, it was really cool to be in New York, and the reason was based on music. Puff Daddy. Biggie Smalls. Tupac. All those people were really important. This was when Bad Boy first exploded on the scene. It was also during the Jill Scott years, and the Lauryn Hill years. It was important to me when I got to New York that I meet a guy from Brooklyn. I figured that such a guy would show me all of the New York things that New Yorkers do.

I met a guy when I was twenty-one years old. He

was very charismatic. And he also had a somewhat high-profile career. He was very appealing because he had a lot of things going for him. He had his own condo. At the time, I had just finished college and was waitressing, trying to find work in the TV world. So the idea of owning anything seemed so grown-up and mature to me. I was a bit younger—not by leaps and bounds, but about six years younger. It was just a very easy situation to find myself in.

We dated for a few years. And then we went on a trip to Miami where he was working. And he proposed to me out of the clear blue crystal sky. We had been living together but had never once discussed marriage. Not even in passing. Not when we attended other people's weddings. Not ever. It really had not crossed my mind since I was still quite young at the time.

But he asked me to marry him, offering me a shiny ring that was really beautiful. It was one of those starlit nights. I said, "yes"—then proceeded to be sick the entire rest of the night. And the next day.

I was in panic mode. We were engaged for nineteen months, and it was a rough nineteen months. We weren't speaking to each other the night of the rehearsal dinner, that's how rough it was.

But we got married, and I can specifically recall thinking that, if I could just get through this marriage for a year, then I would get past a lot of the embarrassment of having had this enormous wedding that my parents had to pay for.

There was one night where it did occur to me that we should not get married. It was the day the invitations were sent out. I remember going up the stairs to our home. He was in the master walk-in closet. He wasn't in tears, but he was obviously distraught. He just said, "I don't want to do this. I don't want to get married." And I remember just looking at him very calmly and saying, "You have to. We have to." I didn't say, "I don't want to." I just said, "We have to" because my parents were spending all this money on the wedding.

I felt that, when you commit to something, you just have to see it through. He was pretty adamant that he didn't want to go through with it. But I think that, after my lovely pep talk, he came back around and said that maybe it was just cold feet. And I thought maybe it was cold feet, too. A few weeks after that, he sent me a prenuptial agreement and told me that, if I didn't sign it, he would not walk down the aisle.

I called my maid of honor and my mom, and said that I didn't know what to do. Nobody knew what to say. We all thought it was weird. There was a very hesitant "just sign it." I remember thinking that this was an absolute disaster. It wasn't my dream wedding. I could go to Mexico and elope, and that would be fine—but there were so many other people's dreams hanging on this moment. So we just kept going forward with it. And it was honestly like watching a wagon falling apart. And I still thought, "What if it is just cold feet?"

At the six-month mark of our marriage, when things had completely fallen apart, we weren't communicating and things were not going well. The marriage had dissolved by six months, but I purposely tried to last a year. I got to about ten months, and then we decided to separate.

The experience of the marriage falling apart was so horrifying to me. My parents had been married for more than thirty years. For everyone I knew, their parents had been married for so many years. When you marry young, it's not like all of your friends are married and you certainly don't have friends who are divorced. It was extremely embarrassing—and extremely painful. I had to redefine who I was, and how I was going to move forward in a romantic relationship.

A lot of it was just about growing up and knowing that a commitment that I tried to make at twenty something was not the same commitment that I would try to make at thirty something. A lot of people do it so beautifully and with such success. I was not one of those people.

After the divorce, I was not thinking about dating,

so busy with my job. Matt's profile was about his interest in politics, his interest in books, his advancement of social climates, and being involved in underprivileged kids' lives. To me, he read like the perfect man on paper because his view of the world was really similar to mine.

I was excited. We must have emailed back and forth five times in total, mainly to find out general information about each other. He was in Brooklyn and I was in Jersey City. We worked about ten blocks from each other, so we made a plan to meet for coffee. At the time, I was freelancing for Viacom Network and producing a daily half-hour show. We planned to meet after work. It was Monday and winter time, a week and a half before Christmas.

Matt was just so warm, cute, and handsome. His online presentation was really him. He was adorable. And I was really happy. I felt like I had made a good decision. It's important to make a good decision when you've made a lot of bad ones. I felt an instant chemistry with Matt.

During our first conversation, I remember thinking that I didn't want to screw this up. I definitely felt a connection with him on that first day. Matt's the type of person that, when you meet him, you feel like you've known him forever. We talked about our families, and about what was important to us and what wasn't. While

I had a superficial job that would impress most people ("Yesterday, I interviewed Snoop Dog."), Matt would talk about an underprivileged child whose parent had died of a drug overdose. He's a grown-up who does things to help people. I do things to make their minds mushy. I remember thinking that Matt was a really good person.

I didn't want the date to end. I usually don't drink a lot of coffee, but he does. I must have had at least three lattes that day because I didn't want to go home. I didn't want it to end being that it was so close to the holidays. We met for probably two hours and then he asked me to go to dinner. We went to this French place in Soho. It was fun. We were the last people leaving the restaurant that evening. That same night, I got a text from Matt. "I asked my roommate if it was okay to text you being that we just met and I didn't want you to think I was psycho. And she said it's okay as long as I ask you for another date this week." So we actually had a second date and I was hoping that this was the start of something good.

On our second date, I definitely had that butterfly feeling of just excitement to be around him. It was a good feeling.

For the holiday season, I was on hiatus from the show and he was on Christmas break from his work. We talked every single day. He drove to Ohio with his dog, and I flew to South Carolina to be with my parents. Matt and I talked on our cell phones practically the whole time that he was driving to Ohio.

After break, I went back to Jersey City and Matt was scheduled to be gone through the New Year. He called me the night before New Year's Eve and said, "I don't know if I'll get a chance to talk to you because you're going out. But have a great night."

The next morning, my buzzer rang. I heard a dog coming up the stairs. It was Matt's dog, Chelsea, followed by Matt. So we spent New Year's Eve together. It was then that we said, "I love you" to each other. It was about three weeks after we met. It all just fell into place. It was a monumental moment. I was really grateful and happy. And in a good place.

His lease was up in August and my lease would be up too, so we thought we had a really great plan to try living together in August. It was a very natural progressive next step. One of the things about living in New York is that you're very transient all the time. Your lease is always for just about a year. It was only January. It just felt really comfortable and really right. We would find a little apartment in Cabo Hill in Brooklyn. We thought this was a really great plan.

It didn't go quite go according to plan. As luck would have it.

Before we could move in together, we planned a trip to visit Matt's family in Ohio at Easter time. He wanted me to meet his family. I was nervous about the trip. I was going to meet his two sisters and his parents, and I hoped they would like me. It's different when you date a guy with sisters because, as another female, you want to make sure that you get along with them.

His sisters were lovely and sweet, offering immediate hugs—nothing to worry about at all. Matt also has six nieces and nephews of various ages. I met all of them. Everybody was really warm and friendly and a lot like Matt. So they were great.

Matt stayed in Ohio while I returned home to get back to work. Once I was home, I discovered that I was pregnant. I had been late for my period but had chalked it up to the fact that I was nervous about meeting Matt's family. Two pregnancy tests, though, confirmed that I was pregnant. But I couldn't be pregnant—I used birth control! I had known this man only three months.

I bought a digital pregnancy test, which, like the other tests, told me in bold, capital letters: PREGNANT. I felt like I was going to throw up—not from the pregnancy but from knowing that I had screwed up again.

How was I going to tell Matt? Our situation was more complicated because I'm black and Matt's white. Matt was still with his family in Ohio. I gathered up my courage and called him. After I told him, there was dead silence on the other end of the phone. He finally said, in the kindest voice, "It's okay. We knew we wanted to be together. We love each other. We were planning on moving in together. It's fine. Don't worry about anything."

Once he returned from Ohio, we met in a park downtown. He took my hand and told me that he loved me, that he wanted to be with me, and that we knew we were going to get to this point eventually. It just came earlier than we thought. Then he said, "I want to marry you, and I think we should get married. You've met my family, and I'll meet yours."

He laid out his heart in his marriage proposal, but, remembering my first marriage disaster, I just said, "no" to Matt's proposal. Matt was not deterred, however, and he said, "We can just go get a marriage license. They're good for 90 days. Maybe we'll plan something small."

I was feeling uncertain about it. Not because I didn't want to marry him, but I didn't want to marry him because I was pregnant. I just didn't want to keep making mistakes.

We decided to go into the courthouse, which was right across from that park bench, and to get in line for a marriage license. When they called our names, it really hit home to me that I didn't want to do this again.

My name was still not my name. I still had my former married name. But we got the marriage license and went back to our respective homes.

I called Matt that night and said, "I don't want to get married. Not today. Not 90 days from now. Not a year from now. I do not want to get married. It's nothing personal. I just don't want to get married."

He wanted to get married and didn't understand why I was so upset. We were expecting a baby together. We had a marriage license, and of course it seemed like the right thing to do. But it didn't seem the right thing to do to me.

Matt and I had ongoing discussions about it. I had morning sickness until I was fourteen weeks along in the pregnancy, and Matt was intent on making sure that I felt well. He didn't want our marriage license to expire, but I did. I just didn't want to get married.

My friend Jessie's niece was turning sixteen and was having a Sweet Sixteen party on Long Island. Jessie and her whole family knew that I was pregnant with Matt's baby. They had met Matt and were really excited about our relationship and the pregnancy.

Matt and I went to the Sweet Sixteen party, and the birthday girl danced with her father to "I Hope You Dance." When the song began, she took her father's arm and they started dancing together. It was a beautiful, emotional moment in time. I was just a mess of tears, and I don't think I was the only one. After Matt and I got back home from the party, I needed to hear that song again. It was healing music, and it was helping me to accept all the changes in my life that were coming so rapidly. Our families knew we were keeping the baby, and that Matt wanted us to get married and be a family together.

The song's lyrics were a lot about taking chances and not living in fear—and not making decisions based in fear.

I realized that some of my hesitation about marriage was really based out of fear of not wanting to make another mistake and not wanting to be wrong again. Listening to the song over and over again really got me to a place where I was okay about marriage again. I could get married again because I was in love this time.

I was about six months into my pregnancy when we finally found an apartment together in Brooklyn. And then my birthday came. My birthday is at the end of September, and the baby was due in December. I wanted to go to the zoo for my birthday. We spent the whole day there, and enjoyed going to the children's petting zoo. We felt like a young family and I knew Matt was right for me. I could do this. I could get married and be with him. I didn't have to sit it out. I could dance.

I didn't want to have a wedding, because it seemed like a waste of money when you have a baby coming that you hadn't exactly planned for. We decided to get married in Vermont.

Vermont is a wonderful place and, at that time, it was the only state that had legalized gay marriage.

We felt that Vermont was a progressive place where people wouldn't look sideways at a mixed-race couple with a baby on the way. The woman who signed us in at the bed-and-breakfast was a woman named Stephanie, and, when she found out that we were in Vermont to get married, she told us that she was an ordained minister and could marry us.

But we also learned that our New York license did not transfer to Vermont. I was embarrassed by our situation because I was eight months pregnant by then. We were meeting other couples on their honeymoons, and I was such a mess. I didn't want anyone to know I was pregnant and not married.

Stephanie made an actual ceremony for us. Her husband Louie was our witness. I picked out an E.E. Cummings poem called "I Carry Your Heart With Me" for her to read. I had Matt's hands in mine and we exchanged vows. It was the most beautiful wedding that I had ever been to. It felt totally right and totally normal and totally easy. And it didn't feel any different than every other moment with Matt, except that it was more special. It was a special moment, but it wasn't scary. I was giddy that I had gotten over my fear. I was exactly who I thought I could be. We felt on top of the world as we drove back to New York, a married couple.

The way I feel about my life now is that it's exactly where it's supposed to be. The goal for every living person is to live within the moment. But that's a really hard thing to do because you don't forget your past. You forgive certain things that happen to you, but you carry it with you and it's your cross to bear. But then you move forward. That's what life is. So here I am now in this life with Matt and our daughter and with another baby joining our family soon.

If it weren't for "I Hope You Dance," I don't know that I would have gotten married when I did. The song helped me realize that I had to overcome fears and I had to take a chance. I'm very grateful because it helped me get to a place where I could be really comfortable in my own skin and make decisions that were not based on fear.

Ultimately, it was the best fairy tale ever.

I'm not exactly sure where music comes from.
I often think it's God's voice
coming through me.

Brian Wilson

(Singer-Songwriter)

Rosemary Clooney's "When You Wish Upon A Star" was the first song I remember that really touched me. She has such a sweet voice and it's such a great tune. From her, I learned how to sing with love in my voice. Music can heal a lot, you know? Not physical wounds, but wounds in your soul. Music can do a lot of good. It makes me feel better to listen to the Beatles' and Phil Spector's records. For some reason, I'm able to come up with beautiful melodies in moments of great despair. A lot of songs are the result of emotional experiences that include sadness, pain, and joy. I often think that music is God's voice coming through me.

"God Only Knows" was a spiritual song, as well as a love song. We knew it was a special love song, something that gets you in the heart. Paul McCartney told me once that "God Only Knows" was his favorite song and that made me feel like a million bucks. I was so happy to hear that. People really liked the words: *I'll make so sure of it*. It was a cooler way to tell someone that I love them. It makes me feel a certain way to know that people, four decades later, are still listening to "God Only Knows" and to [the Beach Boys' 1966 album] *Pet Sounds*. It has really stood the test of time. They like it because it's a good album. It's loving and kind, and it's very giving. It's spiritual.

I think music comes from God. I get inspiration mostly when I'm at my piano. That's where about ninety-five percent of my inspiration comes from. I wanted to write joyful music that would make people feel good and help them heal.

When I was making *Pet Sounds* and "God Only Knows," I had a dream about having a halo over my head that people couldn't see. God was with me the whole time we were doing this record. It all came from my heart. I was inspired to work really hard to make the best record I ever made. Most of the Beach Boys songs were happy and upbeat. I wanted *Pet Sounds* to be something different. [Lyricist] Tony Asher and I were after something deeper and more ambitious, both musically and lyrically.

I think "God Only Knows" reflects a lot about me. When you believe in something, you reflect it in your songs. You say how you feel and the songs don't lie.

Songs are the most honest form of human expression.

The Spirit of Song

Life is lived and that's it.

There's no other way to do it.

In order to really get the most out of life,

you have to move.

And you probably should dance.

Judson Laipply

(The Evolution of Dance/Motivational Speaker)

I began working as a motivational speaker in the year 2000. One of the things I learned early on was a good piece of advice that I got from a mentor. What you have to do is something that nobody else does. You have to have something that sets you apart—whether it's a bit, an idea, a brand, or something else. I wanted to do something at the end of my show, "The Evolution of Dance," that was high-energy and fun, and that incorporated the idea that life is all about change.

A lot of what I talk about is letting go of the things you don't have control over and focusing on things that you do have control over. Just because life isn't perfect doesn't mean you can't enjoy it. And so I came up with the idea of watching a comedian make fun of white people dancing at a wedding. There are a lot of songs that have very specific dances. I thought up the name "The Evolution of Dance" and learned how to mix music on a program. Then, I went out and did the show about a week and a half later. It went over really well, and I remember thinking that this was the type of show that I had been looking to do.

There are thirty-three dance moves and thirty different songs in this show—and I continue to change the ending to include new songs and dances that are coming out.

It's an emotional connection because most of the songs span sixty years of music. At some point, everyone has danced to at least one of the songs and they probably did it at a time when they were very happy. Our emotional memory is six times stronger than our cognitive memory, so most of our positive or negative memories will stick out in our brains much more than the memorization of thoughts and ideas.

So music plays a huge part in our memory. Very rarely in life has anyone been in a place where they were dancing and had a really bad memory. We all had that date that left us or the homecoming day that didn't work out the way we thought it would, but, when we're dancing and we're showing joy, we're happy.

The world is not perfect. Life is not perfect. It has never been, and it will never be. Bad stuff happens to people all the time. Very rarely is our life created by the things that happen to us. It's created by the way we *react* to the things that happen to us. You can stand in front of a storm and you can still dance. You can stand in front of something that you know is not going to be fun and still enjoy life as much as possible.

We do have willpower, and our lives are created by the choices that we make. We're influenced by outside things. But, no matter what, we can metaphorically dance. We can dance internally as well.

One of the things that I love about dance culturally is that it's an expression of emotion. As human beings, we have a wide range of emotions, but our words don't always exactly convey these emotions. Music, dance, and the arts are able to convey emotions in a way that words will never be able to express them.

Authors, such as Shakespeare and other people who are amazing with words, have an ability to convey those emotions but it's a complex conveyance. It takes pages and pages and chapters and chapters in order for them to be able to convey those emotions, whereas music and dance can accomplish this almost instantaneously.

If you would have told me ten years ago that I would make a video someday and that hundreds of millions of people would see it, I would have probably thought more carefully about what video I was going to make, and I would have never thought it would be a dance video. I'm not a trained dancer. I never took dance classes. For most people, I think dance is an outward expression of their own lives. You can either go through life standing still or you can dance.

The first time I heard "I Hope You Dance," I loved every single moment of it. The song conveys so many different emotions. It is a perfect song because it's a combination of everything. It has a great melody, too, that is easy to remember. The lyrics are phenomenal.

Dancing is a choice, and the song is beautiful because it says "I *hope* you dance." It doesn't say that you *should* dance or that you *have* to dance. It's *hope*. I hope you will make the choice to face the things that you need to face, and that you will dance and enjoy that life around you. No matter what happens to you, no matter how tough life gets, I hope you dance.

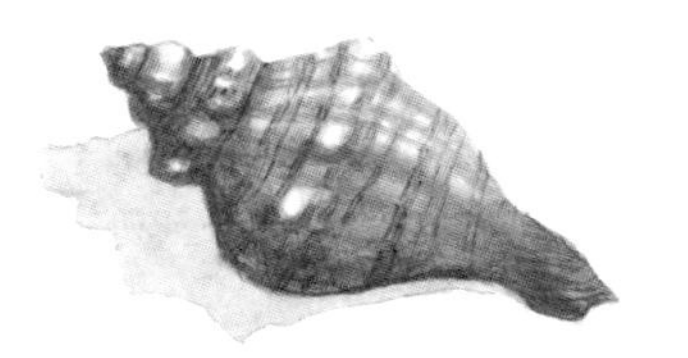

The Power of Song

Music As Therapy

The themes of courage, gratitude and perseverance found within the lyrics of "I Hope You Dance" are at the heart of my work as a music therapist. With music, I help clients find ways to practice gratitude and courage. I use music to heal, both emotionally and physically. I use it to find meaning and points of connection through the human experience. I use melody and lyrics as our tools to uncover strengths and discover new strategies to overcome adversity.

Music therapists are often asked the questions, "Why music? Why is it so powerful?" While there are many answers, the most basic is that music is something we cannot escape. It is within us from our heartbeat and the rhythm of the blood pumping through our veins to the seasons and time—everything is rhythm. We have all had that experience of trying to express what we are feeling and struggling to find the right words. Turn on that perfect song that echoes your internal experience and somehow, remarkably, it says it all.

One of my favorite quotes is by the gifted Hans Christian Andersen: "Where words fail, music speaks." Music is innately a part of our existence.

Music therapists recognize that music often creates markers to our past. In sessions, I like to refer to these markers as composing the soundtrack of our lives. It connects us directly to memories of when and sometimes where we were when we heard a particular song. We can all relate to the concept of being transported by music—whether in our personal lives or while watching a movie. If you've ever watched a movie without the score, it is a very different experience. Without life, we would not have music and without music, life would be dull and inert.

Just as the lyrics in "I Hope You Dance" illustrate, music makes us come alive. Howard Thurman said, "Don't ask what the world needs. Ask what makes you come alive, and go do it. Because what the world needs is people who have come alive." Even at our lowest points, music reminds us that we are alive and that we can have hope when it seems that all hope is lost. Likewise, when life seems to be at its peak—the most cathartic and joyous moments—if music is playing, these moments are elevated even higher. Music amplifies life.

The world is full of possibility, hope and opportunities to come alive. The question often is, "How do we get there?" We dance. We stand up and take a risk. We sing at the top of our lungs and don't care who's watching or listening. Above all, we live and experience life.

We don't sit on the sidelines. Sometimes this is easier said than done, but at the core of the human spirit is the ability to keep going and never lose the thought that there is always something new and exciting waiting around the corner.

Change is a constant in life and music. With this, perceptions can change as well. The way we interpret lyrics, music and life is always evolving. Music opens our eyes like nothing else in the world can, allowing us to hear something new; something we didn't notice before. The lyrics of "I Hope You Dance" could be the words of a mother to her children, a father to his son, a friend to another or a music therapist to a client. These lyrics are universal, malleable, open to new interpretations and yet, still constant. In my clinical work, I have witnessed the song speaking to different clients in very different ways—even within the same music therapy group. Music, after all, is in the ear of the beholder. As subjective as it gets.

That's one of the great gifts of music. It can give you what you need—when you need it most.

Alexandra Field, MS,MT-BC
Board-Certified Music Therapist

Acknowledgements

To John Scheinfeld, thank you for making a beautiful film. For finding these remarkably resilient people who were inspired by "I Hope You Dance." For creating a safe and comfortable space for them to open up and share their stories. For being you. And for loving pie.

Phillipa Sledge, thank you for your passion and steadfast commitment to this project. It simply wouldn't be without you. Your strength, grace, and wisdom epitomize the very essence of the song's spirit. Your love for the arts (and for animals) is just so beautiful.

To Dave Harding and Pete Lynch, thank you for all of your heavy lifting and for doing what you do with precision and care.

To Tia Sillers and Mark D. Sanders, thank you for gifting the world with your song. And for trusting us to care for "I Hope You Dance" in a place far away from the rolling hills of Nashville.

To Graham Nash, Vince Gill, Lee Ann Womack, and Brian Wilson, thank you for bringing weight to the power of song and for sharing what you see, feel, and know about music firsthand. I bow to your greatness.

To Joel Osteen, thank you for offering your perspective on the spiritual side of song.

Tim Storey, you didn't hesitate even for a nanosecond when approached to write the foreword for the book. Your generosity knows no bounds. You sparkle, and I thank you for allowing me into your delightful orbit.

To Hugh Syme, your brilliance as an artist is only surpassed by the sweet gift of your friendship.

To Jackelyn Viera Iloff and Jan Miller, thank you for being friends to the book—and to the vision.

Thanks to Nena Madonia of Dupree-Miller in Dallas; Anthony Ziccardi, Michael Wilson and Gavin Caruthers at Post Hill for their partnership on this book.

Thanks to Esther Friedman, Joy Murphy, Gary Miller, Jody Gerson, Marty Bandier and the teams at Sony/ATV and Universal Music Publishing companies for their belief and support on this project.

Thank you Stanley Hainsworth and Jeff Chavez for your marketing efforts.

Thank you Karen Young for your collaboration on the song's story and even more so for your friendship. We keep connecting dots and by now I shouldn't be surprised—but I still am. I had faith that we would work together again, and am just so pleased that it happened in these pages.

Thank you Deborah Gee for making our time in Nashville effortless and just so much fun.

Debbie Markley, thank you for jumping in to proofread. No doubt Lee Ann will be pleased to have Texas eyes minding my p's and q's.

Music Therapist Alexandra Field, thank you for contributing your lovely essay on music's power to heal.

Kadee Sweeney, thank you for teaching me to dance, literally.

To my wonderful, loving and truly amazing friends—my anchors, my muses, my tribe. Thank you for dancing with me, for giving me wings, for catching me when I stumble or fall. Above all, thank you for sharing every inch of the journey.

To Kelly Mayfield and Nancy Mehagian, our Sunday morning walks are a dance with nature and I am thankful, so thankful, for the richness of those steps, for our friendship, and for the ritual.

Sterling and Morgan, thank you for being you. That's all and that's everything.

To my nine-year-old niece Brianna who would Face Time me with all of the very important news of her very busy little-girl life, thank you for allowing me to step away from piles of transcripts and my laptop to stretch the back and expand the heart.

To Lucas—for being born as I was editing this book, a blissful reminder that the dance that celebrates life is the greatest dance of all. You are a yummy little boy and I hope everything for you and then some.

To my sister, Jennifer, who faces those mountains in the distance with grace and dignity.

To my sister, Mary, who earlier this year wrote three sweet and perfect words in the eye of deep personal heartache: "There's always hope."

To Victoria, Michael, Jason, Alec, Jessica, Patrick, David, Casi, Allie, Caitlyn, Ashley, Dan, Melissa, Maeve, Chloe, Jordan, Jane, David, CeCe, Maria and Quincy: I hope you never lose your sense of wonder.

To my mother, Jean Drumlake, for effortlessly living these lyrics every day and for revealing by example how it's done.

And to my spectacularly loving and sweetly supportive husband, Spencer. We first danced together under the stars in Lake Como just two months after we met. And we've been grooving around the world ever since. More clunkily than gracefully, but there's no denying the joy. And love. So much love! You brought this song home to me one day and said, "Let's do something with this." And we did. Thank you for having faith in me to do right by you and by it. You are a wonder. You are my true north. I love you, and I love us.

I Hope You Dance